THE
GREAT
MAN IS
DEAD

ROB CROSS
FOUNDER OF MURU LEADERSHIP

THE GREAT MAN IS DEAD

A NEW PHILOSOPHY FOR LEADERSHIP

First published in 2020

Copyright © Rob Cross, 2020

ISBN 978-1-912892-86-0

Also available as an ebook
ISBN 978-1-912892-87-7

Cover design by Madeline Meckiffe
Typeset by seagulls.net
Illustrations by Laura Heard Creative
Project management by whitefox

Printed and bound by CPI Group (UK) Ltd, Croydon, CR0 4YY

To my friends, Geoff, Neil and Tom who passed on years ago,
thank you for helping me appreciate that preciousness of time.

To my wife, Candice, and our children Elloise and James,
thank you for helping me enjoy the experience of being human.

To all those I've worked with over the last twenty years,
thank you for helping me realise that the Great Man is dead.

'In the Age of Accelerations, where the pace and complexity of change is unprecedented, our ability to lead through the uncertainty will be defined by the courage and conviction we have in our humanity.'

Rob Cross

CONTENTS

FOREWORD

Shortly after the manuscript for this book was submitted to my publishers, in early 2020 the world was gripped by the COVID-19 crisis. In a matter of a few short months, most of civilisation went into lockdown, paralysing nations, crippling the global economy and leaving many people feeling unprepared, exposed and like they were teetering on the edge of a precipice.

In amongst the immense uncertainty that was created by the virus and the laying bare of our vulnerability as a species, it was absolutely apparent that every human was experiencing increased anxiety. Whether this anxiety was driven by our own survival instincts, or the survival and protection of our loved ones, uncertainty around our job security or our ability to pay the bills, the experience for many was tortuous and unrelenting.

Whilst we all looked hopefully to our political, business and community leaders for certainty and security to help confront this anxiety, many of us found thrust upon us the need to show leadership for ourselves. We were forced to take control of our response to our own circumstance and to stand up and be counted in terms of how we supported our fellow humans. During this unprecedented time of crisis, and in spite of the requirement for social distance, communities seemed to become closer and more connected. For the most part, it seemed that we transcended our differences and acknowledged that we are all human beings, leading and supporting other human beings. And, with our normal daily lives turned upside down, and much of the privilege and simple freedoms we took for granted stripped away, many of us found ourselves questioning our very existence. We took the time to ask ourselves life's most important questions and take stock of our priorities, our purpose, and our very own human existence.

Although I remain convinced that COVID-19 will not be the last existential threat to challenge us as a species, seeing the capacity within humans to show leadership when times are most challenging gives me great hope for the future.

LEADE
IS FLA

RSHIP
WED

'I feel trapped,' Ian said midway through our first coaching session.

As I watched him turn his head towards the window of the room we were in, I could see a mix of exhaustion and sadness in his eyes.

In his isolated state, Ian didn't realise that he was caught in the same situation as many of the leaders that I'd worked with over the last twenty years. He was ambitious and successful in his career, yet he had not reached a level where money was no object. Like many, he found himself in the squeezed middle—he was caught between ageing parents and young children, as well as between a mortgage he needed to pay and an identity and lifestyle he wanted to maintain.

'I feel like I'm running just to keep up,' he said, staring out through the window.

'I'm sure it's just a matter of time before I'm found out,' Ian continued as he turned to look back at me.

'I feel like an imposter,' he mumbled.

Realising that he had never shared these thoughts with anyone, I saw in front of me a vulnerable human being who was desperate for help.

'But, it's important that I create the right experiences for my family,' he said, shuffling to sit upright and justifying to himself why he was doing what he was doing.

I paused, waiting for him to get comfortable.

'There is nothing to rob the human spirit like the rewards of an upper-middle-class existence,'[1] I said, recounting one of my favourite quotations.

Ian looked at me and smiled.

'Ain't that the truth!' he said. 'But I guess this is what leadership is all about … right?'

I looked at him quizzically.

'You know, being the Great Man who has it all,' he continued, looking for reassurance.

I paused, considering my response.

'No,' I replied. 'That's not what leadership is all about. That definition of leadership is flawed because the Great Man is dead!'

Staring at me, a look of confusion swept across Ian's face.

'Ian, if you believe in that definition of leadership you'll live in the shadows of the Great Man forever,' I continued, sensing that we were ready to shift the focus of our conversation.

'Ian, I believe there's a different path for leadership,' I stated. 'And if you're up for trying, I think we should explore that path together.'

STEPPING OUT OF THE SHADOWS

Throughout my career I've worked with leaders across the globe, helping them and their teams achieve higher levels of success and fulfilment. Over this time, by supporting people like Ian and through my own research and experience, I've come to realise that the classic theory of leadership is no longer relevant. Or, as will be described through this book, the Great Man model of leadership is dead!

Each year, focusing almost solely on promoting the Great Man model, companies across the globe spend billions[2] trying to get people to be better leaders with little real change. Asking the question 'who are the leaders that inspire you?' is how most leadership training starts. For those subjected to this training, it often creates a momentary spike of inspiration. But this rapidly disappears as they return to the real world where the pressure of day-to-day life kicks back in, and their feeling of being trapped returns.

'That's great, but I just don't have time for leadership' is what I hear from many people in leadership roles as they try to live up to their preconceptions of what 'being a leader' means. Drowning in a constant flow of information, much of which is just noise, they struggle just to keep their head above water, let alone focus on being the Great Man who has it all.

In spite of all this, the myth of the Great Man continues to be promoted. Why? Because despite its critical flaws, false promises and the inability of anyone to actually fulfil the expectations it sets out, until now the Great Man is the only model for leadership that has existed. I'm sure many people will argue that this isn't the case, but if you look closely enough at these other models, you'll find the concept of the Great Man lurking just below the surface of what they espouse.

WHAT IS THE GREAT MAN?

The Great Man model for leadership is not a recent phenomenon. For millennia, through myth, stories and experience, we've created an image of a leader as being the 'Great Man'; an all-seeing, all-knowing, powerful, heroic character that we put our faith and trust in. Irrespective of gender, race or life experience, the Great Man is the alpha character who we put on a pedestal and who we're told we should all aspire to be. If you don't believe me just type 'leader' into Google or look out for leadership articles or quotes on social media.

Some might say that using the term Great 'Man' is sexist. Those people are absolutely right. It is. And that's part of the problem. For too long across most societies the role of leader has been the realm of the male. However, as I'm sure we've all experienced in our lives, it's not only men who act as alpha characters. Anyone can play the role of being the Great Man.

In spite of the myth that surrounds them, however, the Great Man is not the all-seeing, all-knowing, powerful, heroic character they are made out to be. Regardless of gender, race or life experiences, they are human beings just like the rest of us. Therefore, as a species, beyond all of our diversity, this is what we have in common and what we should celebrate. And with this fact we can realise that as we let go of the myth of the Great Man, we can focus instead on being humans, leading other humans.

A NEW PHILOSOPHY FOR LEADERSHIP

With the classic model so entrenched and without a different approach for leadership, many people in leadership roles feel isolated and trapped in the shadow of the Great Man, much like Ian did. They hold onto classic definitions of what it means to 'be a leader' hoping that it will eventually enable them to 'have it all'. They work hard for promotions, allowing work to consume all their precious leisure time, including their evenings, weekends and vacations. They try to find a 'balance' between work and life while feeling like they're not giving either part of their existence enough attention. They allow the definitions of who they are and why they are here to become corrupted by the dream of the Great Man rather than creating more authentic definitions for themselves. More than anything, however, they forget the Great Man model is merely just that, 'a model', which no matter how well entrenched, can be replaced.

Remaining trapped in the shadow of the Great Man, although perversely providing some comfort, has consequences. As we know, very little grows in the shadows. To grow we need light. To thrive in our lives and achieve the success and fulfilment we are seeking, we therefore need to step into the light by letting go of the classic, flawed definition of leadership. In doing this, however, as nature abhors a vacuum, we need to replace our outdated definition with a new philosophy for leadership, and this philosophy can be distilled into two simple statements:

Stop being a leader

Start showing leadership

THIS
BOOK

CREATE YOUR OWN PATH

This book is not like other books on leadership. It isn't based on some heroic story that is intended to inspire you. I haven't climbed Everest, fought in a war, recovered from any life-threatening condition or created a $billion unicorn start-up company. What I am is an average family man who has helped thousands of people in leadership roles find greater confidence and courage in their own identity, purpose and practice for leadership. I've helped them live with greater mindful intention through feeling more comfortable in their own skin, and through connecting with a deeper sense of meaning and purpose for their lives. And in doing so, I've helped them step out of the shadows of the Great Man so they can achieve the success and fulfilment they are seeking.

And so, whilst this book is not about a hero per se, it is about you creating your own path for your leadership. It is about you understanding what it means to be you as a human being, and from that understanding, it is about you creating a clearer definition for how you will show leadership in every aspect of your life.

This book does not seek to provide a deep theoretical insight or journalistic report on what is happening in the world or on the concept of leadership and how to be a better leader. Instead, this book provides a set of simple yet powerful tools which will help you show leadership in a way that enables you to achieve the success and fulfilment you're seeking both at work and in life.

USING THIS BOOK

This book is divided into two parts. Part 1 sets the context for why a new philosophy for leadership is required. It explains the changes occurring in the world and how these are resulting in the Great Man no longer being a relevant concept. It also explains what it means to be a human being, drawing out the existential drivers of our behaviour—our human dilemmas. Combining knowledge about the changes in the world with what it means to be human, Part 1 concludes with explaining how we are living in a perpetual state of anxiety and that we need a new path for leadership.

With the context thus set, Part 2 focuses on you. It helps you create your path for showing leadership by presenting the 'One Rule' and 'The 3 Questions'™. It helps you let go of your current perceptions of what it means 'to be a leader' and create a definition for your own leadership identity, purpose and practice—that is, who you are, why you are here, and how you will lead and live. It helps you apply the two statements I made earlier and will repeat here. It helps you:

Stop being a leader

Start showing leadership

Central to Part 2 is the Contemplate–Express–Practice (C–E–P) model. As Laozi, the Chinese philosopher wrote: *'To know and not do is not yet to know.'* The point here is that, when you reach Part 2, do not be passive in reading this book. Take time to contemplate what's written and the questions posed. Express what you're taking from the pages by talking to people about it. And most of all, seek to practise what you're learning through trying some experiments.

IT'S UP TO YOU

'Ever the dull alchemist, I have before me all the necessary elements. It is their combination which eludes me.'

Paddy McAloon, singer-songwriter

If you are the dull alchemist feeling trapped in the shadow of the Great Man, and if you are looking to find greater success and fulfilment by unlocking your own and other people's potential, then this book is for you. This book liberates you from the existing, limited perspective of what you've been taught it means to 'be a leader'. It does this by giving you a new approach to leadership. It gives you both the elements and their combination. It's up to you, however, to be the alchemist and bring them together!

This book isn't trying to be a silver bullet. It recognises that life can be tough, pressure is intense and being in a leadership role can be lonely. With this backdrop, however, rather than try to tell you how to 'be a leader' and solve these challenges, it helps you step out of the shadow of the Great Man and step into the light as your self at full potential. It helps you focus on how you can get better at showing leadership in every aspect of your life. To do this it provides a simple formula of 'One Rule' and 'The 3 Questions'™. And through applying this formula it helps you create your path for leading and living with greater authenticity, purpose and mindful intention. This book helps you create your path for achieving the success and fulfilment you are seeking at work and in life.

THE
GREA

DEATH OF THE T MAN

I'd like to say I was a normal kid growing up in country Victoria, Australia. However, when I think about what caught my interest and sparked my imagination, the concept of leadership was always there, which as I look back was a bit odd! Furthermore, as I think back to my classic reaction of 'What the hell?' to the lessons I received on leadership, I realise that I was contributing to the death of the Great Man.

GRENADE IN YOUR BED

The torch light erratically lit up the road ahead of us as it moved in unison with my father's hand. There were so few street lights and so many dark corners. I hated this walk. Every step I wanted to look over my shoulder. But I kept my focus forward, hoping not to alert my father and older brother to the fact that I was scared.

Rain, hail or shine, we walked rather than drove. Although it wasn't that far from home, I always felt jealous of those kids being dropped off by their parents who were less committed to saving fuel and building discipline.

Where were we going each week? Scouts. Although there's nothing remarkable about this well-trodden path, that weekly walk and my experience in Scouts is what spurred my passion for leadership.

'If your men hate you,' my father blurted out one evening after I told him that I wanted to join the Army, 'you'll wake up with a grenade in your bed.'

What the hell? I thought.

Staring straight ahead, I pretended to take in this supposed pearl of wisdom.

'And,' he continued, 'you'll know how much they hate you by whether the pin is in or out.'

This was my first lesson about leadership.

BREAK YOU DOWN

Fast-forward twelve years to July 2000. I was standing there in the officers' mess having just graduated from Officer Training School (OTS), the Royal Australian Air Force's (RAAF) leadership development academy. After suffering through twenty of the most frustrating and limiting weeks of my life, I still struggled to understand why I needed to be yelled at to get me to do the most basic of tasks. The group captain who ran the school shuffled up to me.

'So,' he said smiling, trying to connect with one of the graduates, 'how did you enjoy OTS?'

I stared at him for a moment considering my range of career-limiting responses.

'Do you want my honest opinion?' I asked carefully.

'Of course,' he said still smiling.

'It has been the worst experience of my life so far,' I replied. 'I feel degraded and like I am less of a person than before I arrived. I actually feel like I'm now thinking through cotton wool.'

The group captain stared at me. His smile had disappeared.

'Well,' he replied after pausing to collect his thoughts, 'our focus here is on breaking people down and then building them back up again.'

I stared him in the eye, preparing myself for some corporate rhetoric.

'But I guess,' he continued, 'we don't always build them up to the level they were when they first arrived.'

What the hell?

This was my second most memorable lesson about leadership.

IT'S LONELY AND TOUGH

Fast-forward two years to January 2002. I was twenty-five years old. Stepping into the small, dingy office that was caught between two 1970s accommodation blocks on RAAF Base Amberley in Queensland, Australia, I was ready to take over my first team. I knew the three members of the team I was about to lead. However, with the shortest length any of my team had served being twenty-seven years, each individual had been in the Air Force for more years than I'd been on Earth.

I realised I was out of my depth on day one.

'Can I get you a coffee?' I cheerily asked Darion, who sat opposite me in our little open-plan space.

Darion glared up from behind his screen with a look of distain on his face.

'I drink ten cups of coffee a day,' he said sternly. 'I will never offer to make you a brew and you never need to offer to make me one.'

'Got it,' I replied, quickly scurrying off to our kitchenette.

Great start, Rob, I thought, wondering how long I could hide before going back to my desk.

As the officer-in-charge of that team, my first real leadership role was lonely. I was lost and hated coming into the office. Although I knew all the theory, I just wanted someone to tell me what to do each day to 'lead the team'. Everything I tried was met with challenge, especially by Colin.

Completely unsure of what to do I reached out to my boss, who, ironically, was Colin's previous boss.

'He was like that with me too,' my boss said to me.

'Just ignore him and you'll learn to live with it,' was his advice.

What the hell?

Just live with it? I thought, shaking my head as I left the meeting.

Feeling desperate, I tried to talk to my fellow junior officers on the base. All of them seemed to be struggling but none had any better advice than my boss.

The time came to do the team's appraisals. I couldn't sleep the night before, feeling anxious about how I would handle it. I knew I was in for a tough time.

Sitting in the training room with Colin I started my prepared speech about his performance against his objectives, following all the guidance I'd been given.

'What's your evidence?' Colin repeated after every point I raised.

Feeling my will evaporate, I knew that I was beaten.

Taking a deep breath, I slid all the papers to one side.

'Col,' I started, feeling a wave of anxiety wash over me, 'let me get to the point.'

Col stared directly into my eyes, readying himself for a showdown.

'I've assessed you from two perspectives,' I continued before he could interject. 'One is as someone I can learn from, and the second is as a member of the team.

'As someone I can learn from, you are exceptional,' I stated clearly. 'In the last few months I have learned more from watching you work than I thought possible. I can't thank you enough for this.

'As a member of the team, however, your behaviour and the way you treat me is the reason that I hate coming into work. I believe it is completely undeserved and I believe that it's having a detrimental impact on the team. I do not believe that you are doing this maliciously, but it has to change.'

I paused, still staring Col straight in the eye. His face had dropped, and he looked upset.

'So, what I propose,' I continued with a softer tone, 'is that you and I need to figure out how to work together or you will have to leave the team.'

For the remainder of the conversation Col and I worked through our differences and created a plan for how we would work together.

As I reflect back on this situation, I now know that it wasn't the best way to handle a performance management conversation, but it was the first time in my career where I had to have a difficult discussion with someone in my team.

REAL LEADERSHIP = BEING HUMAN

During the time that followed my fateful conversation with Col I had many experiences in my leadership roles. I'd been responsible for small and large teams, and I'd travelled the world working with leaders to improve their performance and the performance of their teams. In hindsight, I'd like to say that I was exceptional being a leader and helping others, but the truth is I was learning and trying to do the best job I could. Every day I struggled to apply the classic approaches and beliefs about leadership, which seemed foreign to me. This all changed, however, when I received the most powerful lesson about leadership that we can learn. The lesson was this:

We are human beings leading other human beings!

Where did this lesson come from? Quite simply, from my life experience; from recognising that, like all the people I've met over the last twenty years, I have a story which makes me who I am, and which gives me identity and purpose in and for my life. And for me, this story includes the great tragedy of experiencing the death of three very close friends, and the great joy of raising two children with my wife. While none of these experiences is unique, they are a part of my story and they profoundly changed my perspective on leadership. They helped me realise that I am human and so too are the people around me.

KILLING OFF THE GREAT MAN

In recognising that we are humans leading other humans, I came to acknowledge that the prevailing model of leadership—the 'Great Man'—is no longer relevant. Reinforcing this, I came to acknowledge that in today's complex and uncertain world, along with many of my fellow humans, I was ultimately killing off the Great Man. Together, we were killing him through our expectations of greater involvement in decision-making, greater concern for our own and our fellow humans' welfare, and a greater desire for freedom in our lives. We were killing him through our desire to make a difference in the world and through our demands for a different definition of working and living. We were killing him through no longer being prepared to stay in the shadow of the Great Man. And through all of this, we have helped to erode the foundations of his 'greatness' by wanting to step into the light in the full potential of our human selves, even if we didn't exactly know how to do this.

And so today, with the Great Man losing relevance, to replace this outdated model we have created an expectation that those in leadership roles must be humans who recognise that we are all humans too. Therefore, the Great Man is dead, and so it is now our time to start showing leadership as human beings!

PA
CO
IS

RT 1 —

NTEXT

KING

'May you live in interesting times.'

Ancient Chinese curse

As a child of the 1980s, rather than being allowed to watch the cartoons on one of the five channels we had available in Australia, it was the news or shows like the BBC's *Yes Minister* that took prime place on our TV (yes, my parents were strict!). Although I resented not being able to watch the same shows as my friends, in the post-Cold War era I marvelled at the complexity of the world and how leaders like Margaret Thatcher, Ronald Reagan and Mikhail Gorbachev were seeking to bring peace and stability to our time.

From the 1980s to today, I look around the world and it feels much more complex than it did back then. This could be a result of my greater awareness. But I think it's more than that. In the 1980s it was East versus West. Today, it feels like there are powerful, often conflicting and unpredictable forces at play. And these forces are not some distant enemy with their finger on the 'button'. They are forces that we're welcoming in, allowing them to influence every aspect of how we live, whilst at the same time recognising that they seriously affect our health and well-being, and at the extreme, threaten our existence as a species.

As we try to make sense of this environment that we've created, I've heard people throw around clichés like 'change is the new constant' or that we're living in a VUCA (Volatile, Uncertain, Complex, Ambiguous) world. But none of these terms have really helped us get better at managing the environment around us or our response to it. We're still shocked by events, even those that are relatively predictable like financial crises and extreme weather events.

Beyond this, we've also learned more about what it means to be a human being, especially from advances in psychology, medicine, genetics and neuroscience. But again, none of these have really helped us en masse improve how we live as humans. We're still experiencing epidemics of obesity and mental illness, especially amongst the young.

So, if our definitions for the current pace and complexity of change are insufficient, as too are our definitions of what it means to be human, we need something new. My answer to this challenge is as follows: to explain our context, we need to understand that we're living in the 'Age of Accelerations'[3] as Thomas Friedman, the political commentator, calls it, which when combined with the true drivers or our human behaviour, our human dilemmas, creates a prevailing experience of anxiety across our species.

The Age of Accelerations × Human Dilemmas = Anxiety

In the face of this anxiety, we naturally look to those in leadership roles, the Great Man as I have called it, to provide greater certainty about an uncertain future. However, even though our evolution may still program us to look to the Great Man for salvation, today's context is further eroding the foundations on which the Great Man stands, requiring a new and more human path for leadership.

THE AGE OF ACCELERATIONS

The Age of Accelerations x Human Dilemmas = Anxiety

Today, the pace and complexity of change are unlike anything we've experienced before, hence uncertainty is rife. What's worse is that some of the forces which are shaping our environment, and hence our day-to-day lives, represent both causes and potential solutions to the demise of the human species.

Relating this to the organisations that bring necessary employment and security to people around the world, these forces are creating profound changes in the macro-environment, destabilising both marketplaces and operating models. In the face of such significant change, which is driven by three megatrends associated with geopolitics, technology and climate change, it is no wonder that the classic definition of leadership has lost its relevance. And yet, in spite of this, we humans still look to our organisations and their leaders for certainty and security, seeing our jobs as 'islands of stability*' in an increasingly turbulent and uncertain world.

---

* As humans we are wired for familiarity. This is why the vast majority of people feel disturbed when something unexpected happens in parts of their life. To help us maintain familiarity in a world that is changing constantly, we create islands of stability. These are aspects of our life where the degree of change is less than that in the surrounding world. For some people these islands may include where they live or the friends they have. For many of us, due to the amount of time we spend at work each year, work has also become an island of stability that supports our need for familiarity.

MEGATREND 1: GEOPOLITICS

'You're not going to believe this,' my wife blurted as she shook me out of my slumber.

It was 05:34 on 24 June 2016. We were at Center Parcs, a family resort in the British countryside, and miraculously our children were still asleep. Before I could wake up properly, the light from the TV flooded the room.

My wife nudged me again.

'We voted out,' she gasped.

Once our children were awake, my wife and I took turns watching them whilst trying to follow the growing realisation that the UK would be leaving the European Union.

At 07:57 I checked my work email. '*Urgent: Leadership Team Meeting*', was the subject line that caught my eye. The email from the managing director whom I supported as the human resources director. His message was clear.

'In 2008 financial crisis our revenues dropped by 20% almost overnight,' his email stated. 'We're expecting that the Brexit vote will cause the same, so we need an urgent planning meeting on Monday.'

None of the leaders in the business, including me, expected that the UK would vote in favour of leaving the EU, and truth be known, there was little we could have done to prepare ourselves fully for the outcome even if we had.

. . .

In today's turbulent geopolitical landscape, the foundations of political predictability on which the Great Man once stood have eroded. Just by opening a newspaper or watching any news channel, it appears that the geopolitical environment and the way public opinion and public policy is developed is less stable than ever before. Furthermore, fuelled by the intense manipulation of what shapes our opinions by companies like Cambridge Analytica, the political consulting firm, and other less obvious state and non-state actors, we are no longer dealing with rational logic or well-thought-through analysis. Today, we are all caught trying to understand what is real versus fake, and what is fact versus opinion. The consequence of this is that polarisation now appears to be the name of the game, with differences in opinion resulting in steadfast opposition rather than a desire for constructive dialogue and a meeting of the minds. Further reinforced by the growing prominence of identity politics*, this unfortunately also impacts how political manifestos are formed and implemented.

Confronted by such a turbulent geopolitical landscape, many people look to their organisations, their employers, for certainty and security. They want to know that they have a job that will continue to help them pay the bills, regardless of the outcomes of elections and of the opinions they personally hold. However, the ability of organisations across all sectors to establish a medium- to longer-term strategy is becoming increasingly difficult. Public opinion and

---

* Identity politics relates to the ability of institutions to dissect and respond directly to the identity characteristics of a population, thereby appearing to relate more to individuals' needs. Francis Fukuyama in his book *Identity: Contemporary Identity Politics and the Struggle for recognition* explains this concept by describing how the ability to relate on the basis of identity is being increasingly used to influence our human behaviour, especially during elections.

public policy are unpredictable, consumer confidence is fragile and shareholder expectations remain high.

For many in leadership roles, the ability to influence geopolitics is well beyond their reach. As a result, rather than feeling that they're able to set a clear course for cutting through the waves of uncertainty and opinion, many individuals feel they're being buffeted by an unrelenting swell of less well-considered and potentially contradictory issues and decisions. The prevailing mindset of many in leadership roles has therefore changed from 'let's set a course' to 'let's ride it out'.

Facing an unpredictable geopolitical environment, the Great Man leader is now no longer the all-seeing, all-knowing, powerful, heroic character who is able to provide certainty in an uncertain world. Unable to find a path through the unpredictable changes in public opinion and public policy, the Great Man's ability to set clear direction and lead the rest of us into the future is diminished, leaving this kind of leader just as lost as the rest of us!

In summary, *geopolitics = uncertainty!*

MEGATREND 2: TECHNOLOGY

When I was ten years old, I desperately wanted an Optimus Prime, a toy based on the lead character from the movie *Transformers*. After three months of almost angelic behaviour, I'd saved up half of what it cost. Through incessant begging, my mother eventually agreed to take me to our closest shopping centre which was ten miles from home.

'We'll have to order it in,' the nice lady behind the counter announced as she watched my expression go from anticipation to disappointment.

My mother then arranged a lay-by, where we could pay it off in instalments.

Finally, three agonising months later I was the proud owner of the leader of the Autobots, as the good guys in the *Transformers* are known!

'Alexa, what's the weather today?' my six-year-old daughter asked, hoping to avoid taking her rain jacket into school as I'd insisted.

Just as I felt like I was winning the usual morning battle to get the children to school, my wife burst into the kitchen looking worried.

'Do you know it's fancy dress on Friday?' she asked, hoping that it hadn't slipped my mind.

'This Friday?' I replied.

I'd clearly missed the WhatsApp message from the parent class representative.

With a few swipes of her thumb and approval from our daughter, a ladybug costume was on its way to us via Amazon Prime next-day delivery.

Crisis averted!

•   •   •

Having worked through a career in organisations with quite classic operating models and a reasonably stable customer base, the Great Man's success has been enabled by being promoted through the hierarchy. In each role the Great Man acquired greater knowledge and experience, equipping him to succeed in appearing to be the all-seeing, all-knowing leader. Great Men didn't fear change because change, whether amongst their competitors or their customers, was mostly evolutionary. With the explosive development of technology, however, the foundations of operating certainty on which the Great Man once stood have eroded. Whether it is in terms of rapidly reshaping the markets in which organisations compete or the reshaping of how people live their lives, technology is a disruptor that is infiltrating ever more deeply into every aspect of human existence.

Confronted by such a rapid technological advancement, many people look to their organisations, their employers, for certainty and security. They want to know they have a job regardless of whether they are customers of the emergent tech-enabled competitor or regardless of whether the tech solutions being implemented will change the nature of their role at work. The ability of organisations across all sectors to keep up with the rapid advancement in technology is, however, becoming increasingly difficult. Whether driven by 5G, AI, AR, VR, IoT and other two- or three-letter acronyms which are yet to enter the public domain, technology will continue to be a highly disruptive force. Although technology will give companies new ways of grabbing and holding our attention and finding their way into our minds and wallets, it will also begin to radically change how work is done. Furthermore, it will enable competitors, especially tech-enabled small-scale start-ups, to have a disproportionately disruptive effect on larger, more established brands.

Many individuals in leadership roles, struggling themselves to 'lead through the noise', feel caught in the space where they are seeking to sustain returns from their existing business models, whilst also attempting to transform their businesses through adoption of new technologies. And they are doing this whilst remaining on the lookout for solutions that will disrupt their entire market, potentially making them the next well-known business to go into administration. Beyond this, these people in leadership roles are also realising that technology enabled by AI or automation may be on the brink of replacing them altogether. And this is all whilst the device in their hand is channelling an expectation through social media that they should know all the answers as the Great Man!

In the world of rapidly advancing technology the Great Man leader is now no longer the all-seeing, all-knowing, powerful, heroic character, who is able to provide certainty. They're exposed to the same impact technology has as we all are, and they too can have their entire world disrupted by the next tech genius with venture capital backing.

In summary, *technology = uncertainty!*

MEGATREND 3: CLIMATE CHANGE

'You have stolen my dreams and my childhood with your empty words,' Greta Thunberg, the fifteen-year-old climate activist told world leaders at the UN climate action summit in New York on 23 September 2019.

After sailing across the Atlantic to get there, and using only 495 words, Greta grabbed the world's attention. Through her emotionally charged speech she accused world leaders of inaction in the face of the climate crisis.

'We are in the beginning of a mass extinction and all you can talk about is money and fairy tales of eternal economic growth— how dare you!'

• • •

All the historical records show that the climate is changing, and with it is a rapidly growing groundswell of public opinion about what needs to be done. Across continents, we're seeing record heatwaves and more frequent, extreme climatic events. Although in the short term this does not feel as significant as the impact of geopolitical turbulence or technological disruption, over the next ten to twenty years the impact could be profound, influencing where and how we live and the security and sustainability of water and food supplies. The Great Man, once focused solely on the defined targets of profit and shareholder returns, is now confronted by increasing pressure. Today they must not only continue delivering good returns, but they also need to adopt concepts like Environmental, Social and Governance (ESG)* to ensure they are doing business responsibly whilst helping solve the climate crisis.

Confronted by climate change and growing public unrest, many people look to their organisations, their employers, for certainty and security. They want to know that they have a job whilst also wanting to work for a company that has a social conscience. In response to this, some of the world's largest corporations are taking active steps

---

* The concept of ESG focuses on three key factors of environment, social and governance used to measure the sustainability and social impact of investing in a company. Through ESG, companies are encouraged to provide greater transparency in terms of the positive contribution they are making within society.

to go carbon neutral across their operations. They're also looking at ways of making their products more sustainable and to have a more positive impact on society. Although some do this for altruistic reasons, those leading corporations recognise the connectivity of people and the power of social change. They recognise that in any moment, backed by public opinion, a cleverly crafted social media campaign can change the nature of an industry. The 'David Attenborough effect' on the plastic straw industry, following the environmental broadcaster's narration of *Blue Planet II* in 2018, is a great example. Further to this, whilst on the lookout for emerging social movements, those leading corporations are watching the cost of raw materials become less predictable due to varying climatic conditions. They also know that they're being assessed on the sustainability of their supply chains including what materials they should be using. Those leading corporations are therefore caught between increasing climate-based social pressures, continuing consumer demand for choice and convenience, and continuing shareholder expectations about financial returns.

For many in leadership roles, the ability to influence climate change beyond their own day-to-day behaviour feels limited. Trying to continue satisfying shareholder returns and consumer demands for convenience, they also find themselves weary of the next social media campaign which could create a public backlash against their company.

Facing climate change, the Great Man leader is now no longer the all-seeing, all-knowing, powerful, heroic character offering certainty to us all. They are as exposed and affected as the rest of us to the radical changes both in the climate and public opinion.

As leaders in their organisations they're caught in the middle of seemingly insoluble climate change equation and the expectation that they will come to the rescue.

In summary, *climate = uncertainty!*

THE AGE OF ACCELERATIONS = UNCERTAINTY

In the Age of Accelerations, it's clear that uncertainty, which is eroding the foundation of the Great Man, is ever-present. Although any one of the megatrends creates significant and unpredictable change for all of us, when they are combined the interplay between them is amplifying the uncertainty that we must all face. That is:

$$Geopolitics + Technology + Climate\ Change \neq 3 \times Uncertainty$$

Contrary to mathematical logic, the equation is actually:

$$Geopolitics + Technology + Climate\ Change = Uncertainty^3$$

Applying this equation, even if we choose the ostrich approach by burying our head in the sand and trying to 'tune out', news and messages fuelling our sense of uncertainty will find a way into our consciousness. Whether we like it or not, we will get to hear about the impending disaster that's about to impact us. We'll feel threatened. There is no escape. And in fact, deep down, we don't want to escape it. Why? Because as humans it's our human dilemmas that cause us to feel vulnerable and thus experience uncertainty as threat. And as human beings, throughout our evolution being conscious of threats is what has kept us alive. Unfortunately for humans, however, living in a state of uncertainty causes more anxiety than living in a state of knowing that a bad thing will happen. That is, being wired for familiarity, as a species we are more comfortable knowing that a bad thing will happen than we are with being left to guess whether it will happen or not. Uncertainty is therefore one of the worst states we as humans can live in.

For the Great Man in the Age of Accelerations, the foundations of this role have all but eroded. Although as humans we look to someone to 'save us' from the uncertainty and threat we experience, the Great Man is no longer the all-seeing, all-knowing, powerful, heroic character, who is able to provide certainty. In the Age of Accelerations, the Great Man is just like us, a vulnerable human being, surrounded by other vulnerable human beings!

HUMAN DILEMMAS

The Age of Accelerations x **Human Dilemmas** = Anxiety

From the moment we were born, we've been a human being in the world. Although this seems like an obvious fact, there is no instruction manual for what 'being human' actually means, or how to do it well. The more enlightened individuals have researched what makes humans tick, studying everything from psychology, to medicine, to genetics and neuroscience. Others have turned to philosophy to answer the question, 'what does it mean to be human?'

As mentioned earlier, in spite of all this research, collectively over time we've become no better at managing ourselves as humans. Why? Because regardless of all the technical definitions and theories, we've not accepted that being human means that we're magnificent and vulnerable creatures, whether we like it or not. And, whether we like it or not, our existence and how we can live a fulfilling life are more complex matters than can be explained by knowing about the conscious and unconscious or where neurons fire in the brain when we experience different emotions. Yes, we may know about the Chimp*, but that doesn't make it easier to train!

To understand what it means to be human and why we feel vulnerable and experience uncertainty as a threat in the Age of

---

* In his book *Chimp Paradox*, Steve Peters describes the Chimp as being the part of our brain that drives our irrational and impulsive behaviour. Using this metaphor, Peters provides insight and tools on how not only to acknowledge its presence but also how to take greater conscious control of the Chimp.

Accelerations, we need to understand the human condition and what's ultimately driving our behaviour.

As shown in the diagram below, the most common way of describing the human condition uses an iceberg: what sits above the surface is people's behaviour; what they say and do. Below the surface, and what that behaviour is trying to fulfil is called motive, which includes our values, beliefs, fears and biases. It is our motive that develops through our life as a result of the experiences we have.

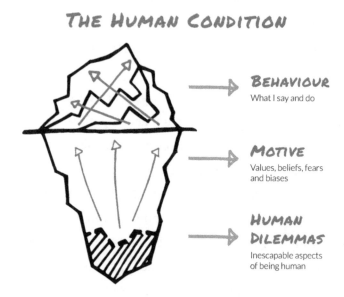

THE HUMAN CONDITION

BEHAVIOUR
What I say and do

MOTIVE
Values, beliefs, fears
and biases

HUMAN
DILEMMAS
Inescapable aspects
of being human

Most classic models on the human condition stop at this point, describing only behaviour and motive. This is why one of the common expectations of the Great Man is to be 'values-driven', because in Great Man thinking we believe that values are the ultimate driver of behaviour. However, as we all know for our own lives, having strong values doesn't mean that we always live by them. For example, most people will claim that honesty is one of their strongest-held values, but these same people will usually admit that they don't always tell the truth!

So, if our motive does not always directly influence our behaviour, what does? Also, what influences the development and activation of our motive through our lives? The answer is our human dilemmas!

As shown in the iceberg, our human dilemmas sit at the core of the human condition and are a set of inescapable characteristics of what it means to be a human. Although the dilemmas are not unique to our species, their combination and the interplay between them is what makes us human. Our human dilemmas are mortality, identity, meaning, freedom and isolation.

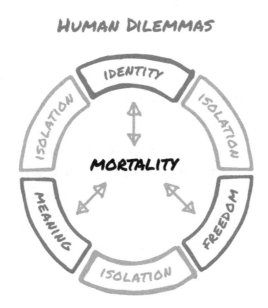

DILEMMA 1: MORTALITY

'Why should I fear death? Where I am, death is not. Where death is, I am not.'

Epicurus

'But ... but ... I've been here thirty years,' the individual sat opposite me blurted out as tears formed in his eyes.

As an HR director I had the unfortunate task of making this person redundant due to a restructure of our business. Although he was a senior director and well paid, and he had a twelve-month notice period which we were going to pay out in full, meaning his family wouldn't end up in poverty, losing his job was devastating. It was as if his professional self was dying.

• • •

As Epicurus states, there's no apparent reason for fearing death. This, however, doesn't mean that we forget about it. Why? Heidegger, the German philosopher, sums it up nicely saying that 'death does indeed reveal itself as a loss, but a loss such as is experienced by those who remain.'[4] That is, it is not the person who dies who experiences the emotions associated with death, it is those who remain living who experience them.

For most humans, our sense of mortality terrifies us, resulting in the need for survival being our strongest driver. To deal with this concern about our own mortality, as a species we've created a range of Great Man-based coping mechanisms. These include believing in our own Great Man specialness: 'You might be in trouble, but I'm Rob Cross! I'll never die!' Or believing in an ultimate Great Man rescuer who will burst in at that pivotal moment and save us before we meet our demise. Or, again positioning ourselves as the Great Man, we may taunt death by actively participating in high-risk activities like running with the bulls or extreme sports. Regardless of which clever tactic we use, however, we need to recognise that they are just tactics. And so, until the experiments of the Transhuman movement* pay off, as humans we remain at the mercy of our biological limitation—we are mortal!

Beyond our physical mortality, following on from the redundancy story above, any perceived threat to our security also feels like a threat to our survival. And what's worse, the concept of losing our job feels like a form of death. However, unlike our physical

---

* The Transhuman movement relates to a collection of different parties who are experimenting in overcoming our biological limitations as a species. As described by Mark O'Connell in his book *To Be a Machine*, these experiments extend from cryogenically freezing, through to attempting to upload consciousness and experimentation with cyborg-style implants.

mortality, this form of professional death sees us still being present. Drawing from Heidegger, Epicurus' quote therefore becomes:

'Why do I fear death? Because where death is, I remain!'

Plagued by our sense of mortality, as humans our focus on survival and security makes us more sensitive to threats. And what's worse, because we're so plagued by our sense of mortality as a species, which becomes more intense as we get older and we have families of our own, we develop a perverse fascination with stories of disaster. This in turn helps keep our sense of feeling threatened alive. 'I did the worst thing any new parent could do,' a friend of mine said just after their first child was born, 'I opened the newspaper.' Another friend of mine said, 'I was a lot more cavalier before I had children,' as he described why he was staying in a job that was eroding his confidence.

Consumed by a concern for survival, many look to the organisations that employ them for certainty and security. They want to know that they have a job that is stable, giving them employment until the day they decide to leave. But in the Age of Accelerations, where the pace and complexity of change is unprecedented and therefore uncertainty is rife, guaranteeing the level of stability and security demanded is not possible. This leaves all workers, no matter at what level, feeling as though the risk of unemployment looms above them constantly. 'It's just the way it is,' a senior manager in a financial services firm said to me. 'I've just learned to live with the feeling of waiting for the axe to fall.'

For many individuals in leadership roles, the fear of their professional mortality creates a barrier for their effectiveness and success. Concerned about 'getting fired' in a time where organisations are in constant state of flux and uncertainty is high, they work within their capability. They try to perform well, but not stand out too far from the crowd. They hear terms like 'fail fast' or 'take risks', understanding their meaning whilst at the same time feeling the threat response that these terms illicit. Their true capability often only becomes apparent when they make the decision to leave, thus proving they are invincible to the forces that may end their employment with the company. 'They got so much more done once they'd resigned', is a phrase I've heard repeatedly in my career.

Like others, fearful of their professional mortality, the Great Man leader is now no longer the all-seeing, all-knowing, powerful, heroic character, who is able to provide certainty. They seek security like the rest of us because they too are vulnerable to changes which, although may not kill them physically, may strip them of their Great Man status.

Facing the dilemma of mortality, the humans who have learned to unlock their own and others' potential accept their physical and professional mortality and the vulnerability this creates. They allow the dark background of death to bring out the tender colour of life in all their purity as George Santayana, the Spanish philosopher describes. They recognise that all experiences are finite, including life itself, and therefore seek to make the best use of their one truly finite resource, time!

In summary, *mortality = vulnerability*

DILEMMA 2: IDENTITY

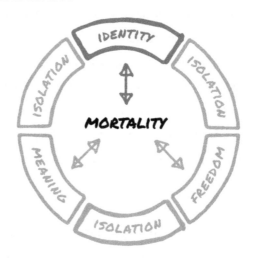

'Rob, can I ask your advice?' the director asked as she sat down opposite me in the private meeting room.

'Sure,' I replied casually.

'I've been told I'm disingenuous,' she said, her hands shaking as she tried to control her emotions.

Before she could say any more, tears rolled down her cheeks. She pulled a tissue from her pocket and tried to dab them away.

In the conversation that followed it became clear that this individual was holding on to a sense of identity so tightly that it was suffocating any display of her being 'a real human'. Drawn from the expectations of her father, we discovered that 'disingenuous' was code for 'too polished'. She was flawless in appearance, presentation and presence. Hence, her team and the business saw her as disingenuous because they could not see the real person behind the mask.

• • •

'Rob, you are expected to wear a tie,' my boss said after a month in my new job. 'And your credibility here will be based on whether you do that.'

I paused, contemplating my range of career-limiting responses.

'When has my credibility ever been based on a non-functional item of clothing?' I asked provocatively.

. . .

As humans, we're taught to be conscious of our identity. Every moment of the day we are bombarded by images and messages telling us how we should look and act. Irrespective of how much we might say that 'we don't care what people think', it's simply not true. We care deeply. In fact, behind maintaining our survival, the next primary driver of our behaviour is trying to influence how other people perceive us. Why is this important? Because as humans we are still tribal creatures who want to be perceived positively by others so that we're welcomed into their tribe. After all, being in a tribe represents safety. Being out there all alone is dangerous, which is why the connection to others via social media, even if not real, has become so addictive.

In response to our concern about our identity, and to influence the perceptions of others so that we remain a part of their tribe, we consciously and unconsciously shape our identity over time. To help us do this we've created a range of Great Man-based coping mechanisms that help us control what we wear and how we 'show up' in terms of our physical appearance and behaviour. We have also learned to attach our identity to the roles and job titles given to us by our employers, relying on these titles as the default answer to the question 'what do you do?' In doing this and seeking to present ourselves as the Great Man, however, we risk masking our true feelings and natural behaviour, pretending to be somebody that is at odds with who we really are. And the consequence of this is feeling like an imposter sitting in the shadow of the Great Man. Regardless of the coping mechanisms we use, all of them are designed to help us create an identity that positions us as the Great Man who stands apart from others, whilst paradoxically keeping us within their tribe.

In relation to the formation of our identity, Ernesto Spinelli, the psychotherapist, describes identity and the associated way in which we view the world, our world view, as being like the sediment at the bottom of a barrel[5]. Over the years, each layer settles and is compressed by subsequent layers, ultimately becoming rigid. Core parts of our identity therefore become fixed because we believe they've worked to keep us accepted and safe. As they become fixed, however, rarely are we aware of their presence or test whether our identity is supporting us or getting in the way. For example, our current identity might help us be accepted by a certain tribe, but is that really the tribe we authentically want to be a part of? Building on from our concern for survival and mortality, although we might recognise that our identity is changeable through choice, we don't always exercise this choice. Even in seemingly innocuous ways, we rarely have the courage to break through rigid sediment to show up in a different way. For example, some people struggle to stop wearing a suit and tie even if the policy is dress-down Friday.

Concerned by the challenges inherent in maintaining an identity that helps them fit in, many people look to their organisations for certainty and security. They want to know that they have a job that will continue to pay whilst also being in a place where they can 'be themselves' and feel included. In the Age of Accelerations, however, where the pace and complexity of change is unprecedented and therefore uncertainty is rife, trying to continually 'fit in' whilst holding onto the sedimented aspects of our identity can be difficult. The fluidity of what is believed to be acceptable in terms of identity and world view within organisations remains high. Encouraging diversity and inclusion has become a mantra for many enterprises, whilst the definition of who 'fits' the culture often still flows with the expectations of the market. 'We might now have more people with different-coloured skin and more people who are openly from the LBGTQ community,' a senior human resources manager said to me in a moment of honesty, 'but the people we're employing still largely think about the world in the same way because that's what our customers want.'

For many people in leadership roles, the maintenance of their identity is paramount. Modern structures in organisations feed off this, creating elaborate titles that boost our ego, and which help us boast to people at parties about what we do, further forcing us to compare ourselves to others. Beyond this thin veil, however, are layers of sediment which represent who we and who others believe we are, including the good and the bad. And holding that sediment together is a fear that if we seek to change, we lose the foundation for our confidence as we face an increasingly uncertain world. In this circumstance it is easy to encourage people to adopt a growth mindset* but doing this often requires us to let go of fixed beliefs about who we are, which we perceive have helped keep us safe until now.

Like others, conscious of their identity and the pressures to conform, the Great Man leader is now no longer the all-seeing, all-knowing, powerful, heroic character, who is able to provide certainty. These Great Men are torn between the classic definition of what 'being a leader' means and a desire to be more authentic in themselves. And they recognise that even though they have become a slave to their identity, in the blink of an eye, the title that maintains their status could be shattered through an unexpected exit from their job.

Facing the dilemma of identity, people who have learned to unlock their own and others' potential recognise the importance of their identity and the vulnerability it creates. But rather than become rigid, they hold their identity lightly, focusing on being clear on who they authentically want to be whilst adapting to their circumstance. They are conscious of who they see in the mirror and are comfortable with that person!

In summary, *identity = vulnerability*

---

* Initially through researching students' attitudes about failure, Dr Carol Dweck coined the term fixed and growth mindset to describe the underlying beliefs people have about learning and intelligence. Dr Dweck identified that when students believe they can get smarter, they understand that effort makes them stronger. This results in them putting in extra time and effort, and that leads to higher achievement.

DILEMMA 3: MEANING

'Why do you do this?' I asked the partner from one of the Big Four accounting firms during our first coaching session.

'Do what?' he asked, clearly confused by my question.

'Be a partner, work for this company, do this role,' I reeled off rapidly to make my point.

'Umm … umm …' he murmured before pausing. 'I don't know.'

He paused again.

'I've never been asked that before,' he finished.

· · ·

'Why do you do this?' I asked the senior director sitting in front of me at a workshop.

'Do what?' she asked, clearly confused by my question.

'Your job,' I stated.

'For my daughter,' she replied without hesitation. 'I want her to know what's possible. I want her to see that she doesn't have to be limited by what other people tell her to do. I want her to follow her own path.'

. . .

As humans, we are meaning-making creatures. We need to have an answer for why things are as they are and why things have happened. In fact, we're so desperate for meaning that when we can't find an obvious reason for 'why', we make it up by saying things like 'it's Murphy's Law' or 'it's fate'. The meaning we create in any moment becomes our truth. It defines what's important to us and directs where we focus our attention and invest our energy.

In response to our need for answers to the question of why things happen, to help us find meaning we've created a range of Great Man-based coping mechanisms. We've learned to become fatalistic, believing that things were always going to work out that way, meaning we have no control over our circumstances or our response to them. Or we've learned to become hedonistic, believing that none of it matters anyway because there is no reason for why things happen. Or, acting as the Great Man, we've learned to shut off other possible reasons for why things happen, instead holding steadfast to our beliefs and never questioning the sense of reality we have formed; 'I'm right and that's all there is to say,' a previous manager I knew would say to his team.

Concerned by the challenges in developing and maintaining a sense of meaning, many look to their organisations for certainty and security. They want to know that they have a job that will continue to pay, whilst also helping them find meaning and purpose in the work they do. In the Age of Accelerations, however, where the pace and complexity of change is unprecedented and uncertainty is rife, creating a clear sense of purpose which guides all decisions in the organisation and which employees can feel connected to, requires significant effort. In recent years, spurred on by the recognition that humans no longer just wanted to turn up and do a job, and spurred on by the growing social conscience and a desire to create attractive recruitment propositions, many corporations have pursued the concept of creating meaning by defining altruistic purpose statements for their activities. In doing this, some organisations have gone beyond a catchy strapline to embed their purpose at the core of what they do, dealing with paradoxical tension of pursuing commercial interest and societal well-being. Others, unable to deal with this paradox, have used their purpose statements to shroud the fact that their real 'reason for being' is just to make money, leaving those who joined for the stated reason feeling confused and resentful when they realise the truth. To help create connection between individual and organisational purpose, the more enlightened organisations have attempted to ensure the contribution of all their employees aligns to their stated purpose. They have tried to emulate the purpose-driven janitor from the famous story told by John F. Kennedy, the former US president. As the story goes, when Kennedy asked a janitor what his role was during a tour of NASA in the lead-up to the moon landing, the janitor stated that his role was to help put a man on the moon.

At an individual level, for those of who accept the responsibility of creating meaning for themselves, driven by preconceptions of what society wants, it's easy to be seduced into creating some form of lofty purpose statement. From this perspective, like a beauty pageant contestant we risk stating that our purpose and legacy will be to create world peace, eliminate malaria or solve famine in Africa. However, if we are honest with ourselves, the reasons we do what we do, and thus what's important to us, are probably in general a lot closer to home; to pay the mortgage, to keep food on the table, to take care of our family, to go on nice holidays, etc. And when we think about our legacy through our work, it's often about the difference we make to the people we work with rather than the difference we make to our customers or returns we generate for shareholders. Rarely, however, have we defined these things for ourselves.

Many individuals in leadership roles, confronted by the need for meaning unconsciously 'make it up', hoping to justify their existence by proving their worth to the business. 'This report absolutely has to get done today,' is a statement I've heard over the years, only to find that just one paragraph from the report gets used, and even then, that paragraph doesn't matter very much. Caught in this false sense of meaning, where the focus is on the minutiae, the real understanding of 'what's most important to me' is lost in a cloud of confusion about overwhelming priorities and a fear that I might lose my job if I don't satisfy what I perceive is important to the organisation.

Like others, struggling with defining meaning and what's important to them, the Great Man leader is now no longer the all-seeing, all-knowing, powerful, heroic character, who is able to provide certainty. The Great Man is torn between what he perceives the organisation expects of him and will be rewarded for, and a definition of what's important for him in his own life. Great Men leaders recognise that if they give less focus to what they perceive the organisation wants, then they are no longer the Great Man. Instead, they are just like everyone else, struggling to balance it all. The Great Man clings on to the meaning that got them to the position they find themselves occupying, fearful for what will happen and what they'll find if they let it go.

Facing the dilemma of meaning, the humans who have learned to unlock their own and other people's potential, recognise their need for meaning and having a reason for why things happen. Rather than feel at the mercy of their surroundings they are conscious of the meaning they are creating and so they create that meaning consciously, allowing them to understand and focus on what is important to them.

In summary, *meaning = vulnerability*

DILEMMA 4: FREEDOM

'Which job do you think I should take?' my wife asked me as she grappled with the quandary facing her.

After leaving a company she'd been with for thirteen years, she now had two good job offers on the table.

'Well, it's your choice,' I responded, watching frustration flash across her face.

Following the creation of numerous lists of pros and cons and seeking the advice from many far more helpful people than me, she eventually made a selection. With the decision made she created stories to justify her choice, all the time plagued by a niggle of whether it was the right one.

One week into her new job, she phoned the recruitment consultant who helped her find the other opportunity to see if it was still available. Clearly, in spite of her decision she was still torn between choices.

• • •

As humans we're free to choose what we do with our time. In fact, our freedom is so inescapable that even when we don't choose, we are still in effect making a choice. Our freedom to choose is therefore a responsibility that we cannot avoid. That is, we can tell ourselves that we're just following the instructions of others, but it is still up to us as to whether we choose to follow those instructions.

In response to our inescapable freedom, to help us cope with the need to choose and make decisions, we've created a range of Great Man-based coping mechanisms. In certain moments we may pretend to be the Great Man, shooting from the hip, never questioning the basis for the direction we're taking. In other moments, to avoid compromising our Great Man status we may avoid decisions, putting them off, hoping that they will just go away. Or, we may seek to abdicate our responsibility by pushing the decision onto others, hoping that they can take on the mantle of the Great Man by confidently providing the answers we are looking for: 'I'm just going to "escalate" this decision,' was a common phrase I heard in one organisation where people were afraid to make decisions and so would push them up the hierarchy.

Furthermore, in support of these Great Man coping mechanisms, much like my wife confronted by the dilemma of which job to choose, we use other, more subtle tools. We seek counsel from others hoping to ease the burden of making a decision. We create lists of pros and cons, hoping to create the illusion of objectivity. And we put decisions off, hoping that the passage of time will reveal the 'right' answer. Unfortunately, regardless of which coping mechanism or tool we may use, for many decisions we face in life, especially those we face in leadership roles, there is no right answer. The choices which face us, therefore, often result in the need for trade-offs, which is why our dilemma of freedom is so confronting. What's more challenging is that every time we make a choice, we negate the other choices. That is, by taking one path, the others disappear. My wife may have wanted to do both jobs, but she had to choose one, meaning the other job was given to another candidate.

Concerned by the challenges in accepting freedom and responsibility, and overwhelmed by the often exaggerated importance of most decisions, many look to their organisations for certainty and security. They want to know that they have a job that will continue to pay, whilst also creating clear boundaries for the decisions they need to make in life, thus helping to abdicate some parts of their freedom.

However, although consciously this results in them resenting the lack of freedom that comes with having a job (for example, not being able to sleep in when they want), often unconsciously they welcome the need to not have to make too many decisions in their life. In the Age of Accelerations, however, where the pace and complexity of change is unprecedented and therefore uncertainty is rife, organisations remain in a constant state of flux. The paradigm of having a stable job or a job for life is over and so the need to make more significant decisions on a more frequent basis is now the norm for many. In the Age of Accelerations, the dilemma of freedom cannot be avoided. The confrontation of choice will always find us in the end!

For many in leadership roles, confronted by the responsibility to make decisions and thus exercise their freedom, they feel overwhelmed with knowing what the 'right' thing to do might be, especially in a world when there is no right answer. In spite of rhetoric like 'fail fast' or 'failure is not fatal', the pressure resulting from their sense of responsibility is compounded by a fear of the consequences if they get it wrong. Decisions get over-complicated, get put to committees, or they get escalated up the chain of command, drawing more people into the obligation to confront their freedom to choose.

Like others, struggling with the responsibility which comes with the freedom to choose, the Great Man leader is now no longer the all-seeing, all-knowing, powerful, heroic character, who is able to provide certainty. The Great Man is operating in a highly complex and uncertain world with no right answers. Their teams, seeking to abdicate their own responsibility, look to them for decisions and direction, which they're required by the organisation to provide. As the Great Man, hiding their vulnerability by refusing to acknowledge that they don't know what to do, they forge ahead as if walking through a minefield where each decision they make could create an explosion undermining their position.

Facing the dilemma of freedom, the people who have learned to unlock their own and others' potential recognise their inescapable freedom. Rather than feeling overwhelmed by the need to make decisions, however, they accept that very few decisions are completely irreversible*, and so apply a more experimental approach, allowing every decision to lead to new paths and new possibilities.

In summary, *freedom* = *vulnerability*

DILEMMA 5: ISOLATION

---

* In response to our inescapable freedom, it should be noted that although we cannot avoid our responsibility to make choices, very few choices in life are fully irreversible. In my experience, the only choice that I've encountered that is completely irreversible is suicide. With that, we can recognise that the pressure we place on ourselves to choose is often more intense than it needs to be. We expect there to be a right answer that we can never rescind, but in my experience across the last twenty years, this is not the case.

'Who do you go to for support?' I asked the executive I was working with.

'There's a few people I can ask for advice,' he replied without real commitment.

It was clear the transformation programme was not going well, and he felt alone and exposed. The 'buck' was stopping with him.

'This is a really complex programme,' I replied. 'I would really encourage you to build an advisory team as soon as possible.'

      • • •

'How are you?' I asked, watching the CEO shuffle uncomfortably in his seat.

'All right, I guess,' he replied.

Sitting behind the small coffee table, the CEO picked up his coffee mug. Holding it in both hands, he stared at the whiteboard that was covered in scribbled writing behind me.

The company was facing another crisis and questions were being asked by the Board about the CEO's future and the capability of the leadership team.

'I never thought this role would be so lonely,' he said, breaking the silence.

'I read that being a CEO was lonely, but I just dismissed it as nonsense,' he continued, shifting his gaze back to me. 'Now look at me. Here I am, stuck between the board and my team. All looking to me for answers and all waiting for me to fail.'

      • • •

As humans, no matter how close we get to another person, we remain a single, isolated human being. It is therefore our isolation that binds our human dilemmas together, because through our isolation we're required to confront our human dilemmas for ourselves, by ourselves.

In response to our inescapable isolation, to avoid feeling alone and lonely, we've created a range of Great Man coping mechanisms, especially in terms of how we create connections with others. We seek to take on Great Man leadership roles, being responsible for teams who are required to pay attention to what we say and spend time with us when we require it. We join tribes either in person or online. And whether they be in the form of groups, teams, clubs or organisations, we hope that through membership we're not left out in the cold. Irrespective of the coping mechanism we adopt, however, just because we join a tribe doesn't mean that our sense of isolation disappears. We can have a thousand friends on Facebook or be the CEO of a 100,000-person organisation, yet still feel alone and lonely.

Adopting different coping mechanisms, helping us become part of a tribe, does help ease the tension created by our human dilemmas. We ease the tensions relating to our identity because we don't need to worry about choosing how we look or show up. We can seek to fit in by just mimicking other tribe members. We ease our need for meaning by finding it in the purpose of the tribe and tasks we undertake to contribute to it. And finally, we ease our sense of freedom by following the tribe rather than setting our own path.

In the Age of Accelerations, however, where the pace and complexity of change is unprecedented and therefore uncertainty is rife, our attempts to ease our experience of isolation and the tension created by our other human dilemmas also has the potential to restrict us. Fearful of our vulnerability in the face of uncertainty, we maintain an identity that helps us remain accepted by the tribe. This, however, prevents us from breaking the layers of sediment that limit other ways for how we could show up in the world. We attach meaning to being part of the tribe and the tasks that sustain it, potentially ignoring what really matters most to us. We let go of parts of our freedom, allowing many decisions to be made for us, all the time resenting the control we feel is imposed, whilst simultaneously convincing ourselves that it has to be done for the good of the tribe. And finally, although we're connected to others, those connections are rarely deep and more often are distracting acquaintances. The energy consumed by these connections prevents us from using our isolation to find confidence in our own sense of identity and purpose and to develop deeper connections with others. Occasionally, we might see a few people break free, setting up on their own or venturing into new tribes, and periodically we might toy with this idea ourselves. However, often we realise that these types of moves are replacing one tribe and one set of restrictions with another.

For many people in leadership roles, when confronted by their sense of isolation they find themselves lonely. Whilst they're a part of the team they lead, they're also removed from it. As Gareth Jones, co-author of *Why Should Anyone be Led by You*[6] states, 'those in leadership roles often find themselves in this close but distant relationship with the teams they are a part of'. Why? Because in the leadership role, the buck stops with them and not the team. They are the ones accountable for progress and results. They are the ones who are required to stand up and be counted.

Like others, struggling with isolation, the Great Man leader is now no longer the all-seeing, all-knowing, powerful, heroic character, provider of certainty. They're out there alone, feeling vulnerable and exposed as they seek to navigate uncertainty. Their teams look to them for direction whilst having high expectations about how they will treat them as humans. Rather than being put on a pedestal by their teams, the Great Man is thrust out into the cold with the expectation that they will find and lead the way for all the others to follow.

Facing the dilemma of isolation, the humans who have learned to unlock their own potential recognise their isolation and their need for connection. Rather than be fearful of this, however, they use the tension between isolation and connection to help them unlock their potential. They do this by embracing the power of the human dilemmas as a source of energy to help them achieve the success and fulfilment they seek.

In summary, *isolation = vulnerability*

HUMAN DILEMMAS = VULNERABILITY

Beneath our behaviour and our motive sit our human dilemmas, a set of inescapable aspects of what it means to be human. In carrying on our day-to-day lives it is easy to try and ignore or suppress our human dilemmas because they make us uncomfortable. It is also easy to dwell on or become fixated by them, worrying about how they manifest in our behaviour. In spite of our potential responses to our human dilemmas, however, we must recognise that they are ever-present, and whether we like it or not, they create a continual sense of unease and expectation. In spite of this, our human dilemmas also provide a source of power to help us achieve the success and fulfilment we desire, but this is only possible if we learn to embrace them. To embrace our human dilemmas means accepting that combination of our human dilemmas, multiplied by the fact that we must confront them as an isolated human being, is what makes us magnificent, vulnerable creatures.

$$(Mortality + Identity + Meaning + Freedom) \times Isolation = Vulnerability$$

In spite of all the encouragement to show more vulnerability, especially in leadership roles, being vulnerable is not something that comes naturally to humans. Why? Because vulnerability exposes us to threats. When we're vulnerable, we open ourselves to attacks and defeat. What's worse, when our human dilemmas are activated in times of uncertainty, if we do not learn to embrace them, our consciousness of our vulnerability increases, as too does our perception about levels of threat we face. A vicious cycle is then created, amplifying the sense of anxiety we feel!

For the Great Man who cannot escape their own human dilemmas, their inability to embrace them is what further erodes the foundations for their role. Although as humans we look to someone to 'save us' from our own sense of vulnerability and threat, the Great Man is no longer the omnipotent, omniscient hero. With human dilemmas, the Great Man is like us, a vulnerable human being!

For the individuals who have learned to unlock their own and other individuals' potential, the sense of their own vulnerability creates an awareness of the risks and opportunities in life. And it is this awareness that they use as a source of energy to embrace their human dilemmas and find courage and conviction in our collective humanity as they seek to show leadership.

THE CONTEXT IS SET

Age of Accelerations x Human Dilemmas = Anxiety

Uncertainty x Vulnerability = Anxiety

In the Age of Accelerations, a new, more radical form of uncertainty is emerging. With this uncertainty directly activating our human dilemmas, the prevailing experience for most humans, especially those in leadership roles, is one of anxiety. Although this anxiety may not show up in clinical form, it is present for many as an unshakeable sense of unease about the future. Projected onto fears about job security, social status, fear of missing out, and a felt need to be permanently connected, anxiety is now directing most people's day-to-day lives.

Recognising this epidemic of anxiety, in his book *Thank You for Being Late,* Thomas Friedman rightfly states that 'addressing anxiety is one of today's greatest leadership challenges'. Friedman also states that 'if a society doesn't build solid floors under people, many will reach for a wall—no matter how self-defeating that would be'[7]. In experiencing anxiety, it is therefore easy, and very human, to close up and go into defence mode. However, this prevents us from unlocking our own potential and the potential of those around us. It prevents us from achieving the success and fulfilment we are seeking.

With context being king, the combination of the Age of Accelerations and our human dilemmas mean that the landscape for leadership has changed. The foundations on which Great

Man leaders once stood and from which they have exerted their power have crumbled, leaving them as lost as the rest of us. For those who want to unlock their own and other people's potential, it has paved the way for them to create a new path where they establish a stronger foundation for their leadership identity, purpose and practice.

PART 2 -
CREATIN
NEW PAT
LEADER

G YOUR

H FOR

SHIP

A NEW PHILOSOPHY

In the Age of Accelerations, the continual stream of uncertainty is hyper-activating our human dilemmas and heightening our sense of vulnerability. To help us deal with the prevailing experience of anxiety that results, we recognise that a new philosophy for leadership is required. Why? Because firstly, unable to respond to the unprecedented complexity and change in our environment and the rapidly evolving expectations of humans, the Great Man model of leadership is collapsing. And secondly, because the individuals who have learned to unlock their own and other people's potential have done so through embracing the human dilemmas. They have learned to use the drivers of their human behaviour to help them achieve the success and fulfilment they seek.

This new philosophy, which enables those humans to create a new path for their leadership, is described in the following two statements:

Stop being a leader

Start showing leadership

Through these two statements we learn to let go of our existing, limiting beliefs about leadership and what it means to 'be a leader'. We kill off our over-dependency on the model of the Great Man, prompting us to 'stop being a leader' so that we can 'start showing leadership' as humans leading other humans.

How do we bring these two statements to life?

How do we create this path for how we show leadership?

We use One Rule and 'The 3 Questions'™.

STOP BEING A LEADER = ONE RULE

'This is Rob, he's an expert on leadership,' is how I was introduced by the host at networking event in London.

The crowd was an eclectic mix. Everyone from investment bankers to artists to CEOs, and a couple of founders of tech start-ups. And then there was me … the expert on leadership!

Standing in front of two ladies to whom I'd just been introduced, I felt uncomfortable. This type of networking isn't really my scene and I wasn't sure about why I'd been invited.

'Leadership is broken,' one of them exclaimed, trying to throw down a gauntlet, clearly unhappy that they were talking to me rather than someone who was, in their eyes, more important.

'I agree,' I said, without either of them taking any notice.

'People think Jack Welch was a great leader,' the first lady continued. 'I worked for him in the 80s and we were all scared of him.'

As I nodded in agreement, the second lady cut in before I could give my view.

'Yeah,' she started, 'everyone says how great a leader Steve Jobs was, but he was a bully. Just because he was a genius, it didn't make him a great leader or a nice human being.'

Still nodding, my opportunity to speak had arrived.

'I agree,' I said again.

They looked at me with surprise.

'The current philosophy on leadership is broken, and that's why I'm going to replace it.'

STEP OUT OF THE SHADOWS

Too much of the current approach to developing leaders involves encouraging us to emulate others. 'Who are the leaders that inspire you?', or some other similar question, remains the most common starting point for the leadership training I've seen.

When we focus on leadership starting from 'who inspires you', we instantly put ourselves in the shadow of others. We also fall into the trap of believing that leadership again is about being the Great Man that we should all aspire to be.

Beyond this starting point, most leadership training moves from this to learning about behaviour, including what they believe leaders should do and say. Occasionally it dips into leadership values and beliefs, or baffles people with neuroscience, but even then, it doesn't help people understand what it means to be human and how to unlock true human potential. It doesn't help them embrace and use the human dilemmas.

The consequence of this current approach is that we create a 'house built on sand'. That is, whilst the description of what we should do and say might be OK—the house—we've not built the foundations for these behaviours in terms of our sense of identity and purpose for how we show leadership. Thus, when the pressures of the Age of Accelerations kick in and our human dilemmas become activated, the foundations crumble and the house collapses. We go from being the Great Man to being an anxious wreck!

Stepping out of the shadows means that we stop applying the current approach to leadership. That is, we stop trying to emulate others and we let go of classic definitions of what it means to 'be a leader'. Through this, we give ourselves space to create a new definition of leadership about ourselves and for ourselves.

AT THE EDGE

With the Great Man model losing its relevance, we step up to the edge of a precipice in terms of what 'being a leader' really means. Standing at any threshold like this, letting go and taking a leap is daunting, especially when our beliefs are so deeply ingrained in our psyche. The Great Man role isn't just something we've created recently; it's been our definition of leadership for thousands of years. In spite of this, we have to be prepared to take the leap. We have to let go of what we've been told 'being a leader' means so we can create the space for a new approach.

How do we let go? How do we 'stop being a leader'? The answer is simple. Firstly, we switch off our autopilot with respect to leadership. Then, we take the leap by letting go of our current definition. And, through this, we find space to create our own path for showing leadership; we find space to apply the second statement of our new philosophy.

SWITCH OFF AUTOPILOT

Much like trying to escape hearing about the megatrends in the Age of Accelerations, it is almost impossible to avoid the reinforcing messages about needing to be the Great Man leader. Whether it's embedded in our job titles through terms like 'leader', 'director', 'head of', 'manager' or 'chief', or it's embedded in processes like performance appraisal, our organisational constructs reinforce the myth that in our part of that world, we need to be a Great Man. We need to be the 'leader of our team', the one who has the power to set direction, provide answers and judge others' performance, deciding where they are on some form of matrix. We need to be the one who decides whether individuals get a pay rise or not. This is all whilst, deep down, we recognise that we're often no more qualified to make these types of judgements than those in our team.

Beyond our organisations we are also constantly bombarded by images and quotations telling us what 'being a leader' means. Whether associated with celebrities, politics, charities or business, as a society we are adept at putting people onto pedestals so we can marvel at their supposed greatness whilst at the same time putting ourselves in their shadow. In this form, as described by Ernest Becker, author of *The Denial of Death*,[8] we create leaders as figures on whom we seek to transfer our feelings about a need for authority and control. That is, through transference, we seek to ease some of the tension created by our human dilemmas by following the direction of the Great Man, allowing him to control what we do and when we do it.

When we're not aware of the unrelenting and pervasive nature of the stories about needing to be a Great Man, they infiltrate our unconscious, causing feelings of inadequacy and insecurity and making us feel as if we're an imposter. We get hung up on what we're not doing, rather than acknowledging what we are good at and the actual difference we are making to those around us. Thus, we stay in the shadows of the Great Man figures, feeling unable and unwilling to step out. 'I can never be that,' someone once said to me during one of our workshops when they explained what they thought being a leader meant.

To switch off autopilot with respect to leadership we first have to understand how our autopilot works. Many people don't realise that the brain is the most energy-consuming organ in the body, using up to 20% of our daily energy. This is why we spend much of our waking lives living on autopilot. That is, if consciously thinking requires so much energy, then it's better to do things instinctively because it uses less energy. Running on autopilot is therefore our way of conserving energy each day. However, when autopilot is switched on for particular topics, like leadership, we don't challenge what we're seeing or hearing. We don't assess the usefulness of the stories and messages that are embedded in our conscious and unconscious thoughts. We allow our autopilot to direct us, rather than taking back control for ourselves and our lives.

To step out of the shadows of the Great Man, it's now time to switch off our autopilot with respect to leadership. It's time to 'Stop being a leader', which means applying this statement as the 'One Rule':

SOMETHING TO TRY:

Now you're aware of the Great Man and how this role shows up in your own life, it's time to switch off autopilot. For the next few days, try noticing all the messages you hear and see about leadership and ask yourself what lessons they're giving you. Notice when you're standing in the shadows of others through your perception of their greatness. Don't judge the messages or the feelings that go with what you notice, just notice them. With autopilot off it's amazing what we see.

LET GO AND TAKE THE LEAP

'Do you mean I don't need to be like them?' the managing director who I was coaching said to me.

'That's right, you don't,' I responded.

'I don't have to be really tough and directive all the time?' he continued.

'No,' I responded.

'I don't have to know about every little detail?' he asked, as his frustrations started to show.

'Not unless you want your team to believe you don't trust them,' I responded.

A look of relief swept across his face.

'So, I don't need to be a ruthless dictator,' he laughed.

'Apparently not,' I replied, smiling, pleased that the point had been made.

It seemed that, for his entire career, this man had been trying to live up to some belief about what 'being a leader' meant. And this belief was based on the behaviour of his previous bosses. He was now ready, as Elsa in the Disney movie *Frozen* says, to 'let it go!'

. . .

To let go of our current definition of what it means to 'be a leader', we first need to understand what our definition is. Rarely outside the walls of a training room do people sit down and capture what they think being a leader means to them. However, without doing this it is difficult to let go of what is not helping us achieve the success and fulfilment we are seeking.

> **SOMETHING TO TRY:**
>
> Whether you grab a pen or just give it some deep thought, consider the following:
>
> - What's your definition of leadership?
> - What do you think it means to be a leader?
>
> and
>
> - Where has the definition come from?
>
> Once you've given this some thought, consider which parts of your definition are helpful to you in terms of enabling you to achieve the success and fulfilment you are seeking, and which are unhelpful.

With our autopilot switched off and our current definitions captured, we can then start to let go properly. Why? Because like any bad habit, when we consciously recognise things that aren't helping us achieve the success and fulfilment we're seeking, we can more consciously let them go!

START SHOWING LEADERSHIP = 'THE 3 QUESTIONS'™

Through the One Rule, which helps us 'Stop being a leader', we dispel and let go of the myths of what we are classically told it means to 'be a leader'. We recognise the limitations of the Great Man model and give ourselves head space—time and energy—to apply the second statement: Start showing leadership.

The reason the first statement gives us this mental space is because we free ourselves of the insecurities and hang-ups that consume us when we exist in the shadow of the Great Man. We allow ourselves to step into the light as a whole human being, leading other human beings. And we step into the light as the person we are at work, at home and in all roles that we play across our life. Now in the light, in order to create our own path as we seek to 'Start showing leadership' we need to answer 'The 3 Questions'™.

Although simple, 'The 3 Questions'™ are powerful because they allow us to embrace and use the human dilemmas. That is, because the human dilemmas are ever-present their influence cannot be avoided. So, rather than suppress the human dilemmas or dwell on them with an unhealthy fixation, we should learn to use them as a source of energy as we start to create our path for showing leadership. And the way we do this is through answering 'The 3 Questions'™.

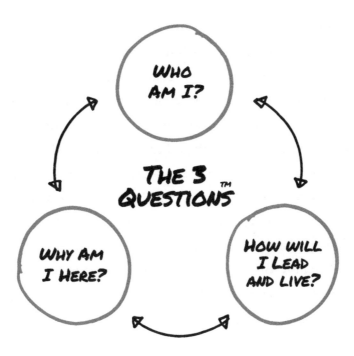

Before we answer 'The 3 Questions'™, however, we need to understand one final thing: the paradox of self-awareness.

THE PARADOX OF SELF-AWARENESS

'Leaders need to develop their emotional intelligence' has been the cry from many leadership theorists over the years. What this means in practice is that they must develop their self and social awareness so they can get better at regulating their own behaviour.

Whilst I agree with the central premise that those in leadership roles need to develop greater emotional intelligence, often the self-awareness part isn't the issue. They're already aware, which is why the Age of Accelerations and the activation of the human dilemmas are resulting in anxiety. The issue for many with higher self-awareness is that this awareness is too often focused on comparing themselves to others rather than being directed towards creating an authentic definition of their identity, purpose and practice for showing leadership. That is, as humans we are social creatures, which means we exist in relation to the others who are in and beyond our tribe. As we seek to develop our self-awareness, therefore, we are always encouraged to take a reference that we can use as a point of comparison to ourselves. And, unfortunately, the reference point is almost always the Great Man, hence the paradox of self-awareness.

The paradox of self-awareness states that between the two levels, our self-awareness inhibits our success and fulfilment rather than enabling it.

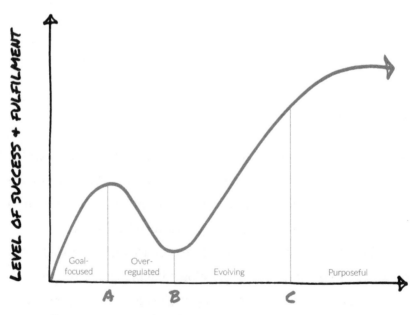

Up to point A in the diagram, we see that growing levels of self-awareness help individuals achieve success. And often at point A, success is defined materialistically in terms of job title and salary, and all the trappings that go with that. This goal-focused level of self-awareness is where the individual understands what he or she needs to do to achieve 'success' and then focuses solely on that. This is the place of the Great Man. And as we know for the Great Man, often their awareness doesn't extend to the impact they have as they seek to deliver on the goal. This is why we often see them at the top of organisations, because their goal-focused approach has allowed them to 'bulldoze' over others, meaning they get things done, stand out and get promoted. 'Dan delivers,' the executive said to me. 'He may upset a few people along the way, but he delivers. That's why he's getting promoted.'

From point A to point B is where the paradox kicks in, and this is where I believe the vast majority of people in leadership roles sit. As John Lawler, lecturer in leadership and management, says, 'reflective self-awareness is a necessary but potentially paralysing force'[9]. In this over-regulated area, individuals are far more aware of how they appear and are therefore very conscious of how they believe others perceive them. With the anxiety resulting from the fear of not fitting in and hence being cast out of the tribe, they over-regulate their behaviour. What's worse, in seeking to over-regulate, they maintain their reference point as the Great Man for what they should aspire to. Why? Because this remains the prevailing definition of leadership and what many people still believe success means in society. However, if individuals in the over-regulated space don't let go of their preconceptions of needing to be the Great Man by moving past point B, they get trapped. They live in a state of perpetual anxiety, each day feeling like an imposter just waiting to be found out.

Letting go of feeling the need to compare themselves to the Great Man and taking the leap created by the One Rule allows individuals to move through point B. In doing this they start to create a new path for showing leadership. They identify what success and fulfilment mean for them, as opposed to what they believe it should be. And then, through 'The 3 Questions'™, they consciously evolve their leadership identity, purpose and practice until they reach a new purposeful definition for how they will show leadership in every aspect of their lives.

Through the paradox of self-awareness, we recognise that simple rhetoric like 'leaders need to develop their emotional intelligence' only serves the Great Man model of leadership. However, if we apply the One Rule which brings to life the first statement of 'Stop being a leader', then we allow ourselves to consciously evolve our identity, purpose and the practice for showing leadership. And we do this through answering 'The 3 Questions'™ of:

Who am I?

Why am I here?

How will I lead and live?

QUESTION 1: WHO AM I?

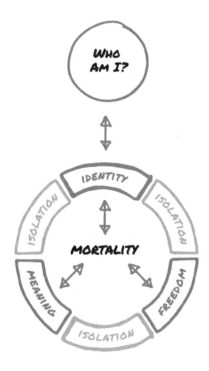

Standing there on the stage, his 6'4" frame already towering above his team, the air commodore peered over the top of his glasses.

'Does anyone disagree with that?' he asked in a sharp tone.

Not on your life, I thought as I looked around the room, watching each of the fifty senior officers around me freeze into statues.

As we left the meeting, one of the air commodore's direct reports, a group captain, cornered me.

'You've got to talk to him, Rob,' he said.

'Why me, sir?' I asked, deeply aware of the *very* big gap in rank between myself and the air commodore.

'Because he trusts you,' was the direct response.

At that time in the Air Force it was my job to help the senior officers in the region make sense of their role as leaders, which, considering the challenges I was having with my team, was ironic, to say the least.

Later that day I knocked on the air commodore's door. He looked up immediately from the paper he was reading.

'Got five minutes, sir?' I asked.

'Sure,' he replied, pushing back in his chair.

Walking into the room, I closed the door to his office behind me.

'One of those conversations is it, Rob?' he asked as I made my way to the wooden chair in front of his desk.

Sitting down, I figured that I should just say what I was thinking.

'Sir,' I started, 'this morning, when you asked "does anyone disagree with that?" did you really mean "I want your ideas and opinions"?'

The air commodore looked at me quizzically.

'Of course,' he responded, seemingly confused as to why I would ask such a question.

'Well,' I replied, my hands sweaty knowing that he'd posted one of my friends to the middle of nowhere for doing something minor a few months earlier, 'it's not how it came across.'

In the conversation that followed we discussed how he was perceived by his team and how we might try some different approaches to get the most out of people.

As I went home that night, I felt chuffed, patting myself on my back for doing such a great job.

I've made a real difference to him and his team, I thought.

Still feeling pleased with myself, the next day I walked up to the officer's mess for lunch only to be greeted by the group captain at the entrance.

'Have you seen his email?' the group captain asked.

'No,' I replied, the look on the group captain's face causing my self-adulation to evaporate.

'He's written to his whole top team,' the group captain continued. 'He's stated that "Rob Cross has told me exactly what you think of me" and that he "demands that we tell him our ideas or there'll be consequences".'

'My chat with him worked well then!' I remarked, rolling my eyes as we turned to go inside for lunch.

The moral of the story: *How we show up is what people will talk to!*

● ● ●

START WITH WHO

Simon Sinek, one of my favourite authors, says that we should 'start with why'. I disagree. As we learn from the human dilemmas I have described, what truly drives our behaviour is in a constant state of flux, leaving us with a perpetual feeling of vulnerability. When mixed with the uncertainty resulting from the megatrends in the Age of Accelerations, our vulnerability creates for us an ongoing experience of threat and anxiety.

Further to this, through understanding the human dilemmas we recognise that beyond mortality, our identity and thus our concern for how we show up and how we present ourselves, is the next strongest driver of our behaviour. Why? Because our concern for how we're perceived by the tribe is critical to us. It is safer to 'fit in' and be part of the tribe than it is to be cast out from it.

To create a new path for how we show leadership we must therefore start with 'Who am I?' because it is through this question that we establish a more authentic definition for ourselves, which then forms the foundation for the two remaining questions.

BEING AUTHENTIC

Contemplating and answering the question of 'Who am I?' helps us embrace the human dilemma of identity. It helps us create a path for establishing a more authentic identity for who we see in the mirror each day and how we present ourselves as we seek to show leadership. It helps us be comfortable in our own skin.

Like many other buzzwords that management and leadership theorists use, the concept of authenticity has become heavily distorted. 'Leaders need to be authentic,' is another message we hear from those 'teaching us' how to lead. 'OK then,' most people in leadership roles respond, 'but how do we do that?'

Authenticity = Honesty + Congruency

As the equation states, authenticity is a combination of being honest with ourselves about who we want to be and ensuring there is congruence in terms of that also being how others experience us. That is, for there to be honesty we must accept what our true strengths and skills are, and in what areas we're not so strong.

For there to be congruence, our belief about how we behave and the impact we have must be congruent with the experience that others have of us. With this definition it is possible to be an authentic tyrant if that is who we honestly want to be and that is how others experience us. What is not authentic is believing that we are a focused, yet caring human being whilst others experience us as a tyrant.

HONESTY AT ALL LEVELS

To answer the question of 'Who am I?' and thus commence establishing a more authentic identity for ourselves, we need to recognise that our identity is not static or one-dimensional. There are multiple levels to our identity that are in a continual state of flux. Authenticity therefore only comes from being honest with ourselves at each level, in each moment.

To establish honesty when answering the question of 'Who am I?' we need to consider who we authentically want to be across four levels: Physical, Social, Personal and Spiritual*.

Level 1: Physical—this relates to how we authentically feel about our physical self and our physical surroundings. Considering this helps us explore how we feel about our health and fitness as well as how we present ourselves. It also helps us explore how we feel about where and how we live, including our possessions and surroundings.

---

* The four levels are adapted from Emmy van Deurzen's work on the dimensions of existence captured in her book *Existential Perspectives on Coaching*.

'*I looked in the mirror and realised that I was in the worst shape of my life,*' a coaching client once said to me. This statement about their physical self led him to start a new health regime that got him back into shape.

'*I can never find anything at home due to the mess,*' another coaching client said. '*It drives me crazy and really stops me getting things done.*' These statements about her surroundings led her to create a new habit of tidiness that allowed her to be more structured and effective across all aspects of her life.

Exploring the physical level therefore helps us be honest with ourselves about the person we see in the mirror and the physical world we exist within. It helps us consider how this is shaping 'who we are', giving us focus for how we use our physical level to achieve the success and fulfilment we are seeking.

Level 2: Social—this relates to how we authentically feel about our relationships with others, including our sense of belonging and acknowledgement. Considering this helps us explore how we feel about our connection with family, friends and colleagues, including how we feel about what others contribute to us and what we contribute to them.

'*I don't feel appreciated by my manager,*' the senior leader said when I asked what was troubling him. This statement led him to proactively seek feedback and recognition from his boss, which helped him feel more confident and appreciated.

'*I feel like all I do is give support to others, and get nothing in return,*' the mid-level leader said after expressing that she felt exploited. This statement led her to consider what support she needed and be more proactive in asking for it. '*You always seem so confident,*' one of her colleagues told her. '*I never realised you needed my help.*'

Exploring the social level therefore helps us to be honest with ourselves about our relationships with others. It helps us to consider the quality of our relationships and how they are shaping 'who we are', giving us focus for how we use our social level to achieve the success and fulfilment we are seeking.

Level 3: Personal—this relates to how we authentically feel about being ourselves, including the thoughts, fears, memories and beliefs we have about ourselves. Considering this helps us explore what we like and dislike about ourselves, and how the secrets we hold about ourselves affect us.

'*I'm just not a confident person,*' the leader said as we explored what was preventing her from volunteering for a new opportunity. Sharing this allowed us to challenge this belief and create a new story for how she felt about herself. Through this new story she ignored the existing opportunity and pursued a different one which helped her better serve what was most important to her.

'*The new people being recruited into the team are a lot better than I am,*' the partner said, explaining what was happening in the team. Sharing this allowed us to explore and challenge the evidence that he was relying on to make this judgement. Through recognising the belief wasn't well-founded, he stopped subordinating himself to his new colleagues.

Exploring the social level therefore helps us be honest with ourselves about how we feel about being us. It helps us consider the quality of our relationship with ourselves and how this is shaping 'who we are'. This gives us focus for how we use our personal level to achieve the success and fulfilment we are seeking.

Level 4: Spiritual—this relates to how we authentically feel about our sense of purpose and meaning that we hold in and for our life. Considering this helps us explore what is important to us and where we focus our attention and energy each day.

'*My family is most important,*' the marketing director said in response to my question. '*But I rarely see them because I work so hard.*' These statements allowed us to challenge the assumptions that were driving her workload and enabled her to shift where she was focusing her energy so she could spend more time at home.

'*I really want to be a CEO,*' the senior director said in response to my question about her ambition. This statement allowed us to explore her true ambition for her life and what was underpinning this. Although her ambition to become a CEO did not change, the desire to make a more positive contribution through the role became her guiding purpose.

Exploring the social level therefore helps us be honest with ourselves about what is most important to us. It helps us consider our sense of meaning and purpose and how this is shaping 'who we are'. This gives us focus for how we use our spiritual level to achieve the success and fulfilment we are seeking.

When considering each of the four levels, through adding the word 'authentically' we're forced to be honest with ourselves rather than answering from a place of preconception. Through the word 'authentically' we are also given direction about where we want to improve ourselves. That is, if we get to the core of how we 'authentically' feel, then we can decide if that's how we authentically *want* to feel. When the answer is 'no' or 'not that', then we have no excuse but to take action. For example, accepting that 'I don't authentically want to feel like I'm not good enough' gives us a clear direction for action.

Through recognising the levels of identity and answering the question of '*how do I authentically want to feel about ... ?*' we can bring clearer direction and detail to the definition of our authentic identity. Furthermore, by being honest with ourselves we can avoid trying to live up to preconceptions of what we think the answers should be, and instead, we can look deep within us and discover what is right for us. It is this which ultimately allows us to become more comfortable in our own skin.

CONGRUENCE AT ALL LEVELS

Building on being honest with ourselves at all levels, when answering the question of 'Who am I?', we also need to acknowledge the congruency element of the authenticity equation: how do people experience us? That is, are people actually experiencing us in the way we want them to?

Why is this important? Because, as we know, how we appear is ultimately what people will respond to. To reinforce the point: many years ago, I had a manager who would respond in exactly the same way every time someone presented them with an idea. 'That's not how I see it,' he would say without hesitation, believing that he was an empowering leader. Very rapidly, people stopped coming to him with ideas because we all realised that clearly no one could be as smart as the Great Man!

Acknowledging the congruency element means we should be conscious, but not obsessed by how we appear to others. Again, the four levels help us here:

- *Level 1: Physical*—how do we authentically want people to experience us through our physical presence?
- *Level 2: Social*—how do we authentically want people to experience us in our relationship with them?
- *Level 3: Personal*—how do we authentically want people to experience us in terms of how we feel about ourselves?
- *Level 4: Spiritual*—how do we authentically want people to experience us in terms of what is important to us?

Bringing together our honesty and congruency responses allows us to not only be honest with ourselves about who we want to be across each of the four levels, it also allows us to consciously focus on making sure that is how people experience us.

OVER TO YOU ...

Answering the question of 'Who am I?' isn't about our personal brand or creating some catchy three-word strapline for our identity, like 'Just do it'; that's Great Man thinking. It is about gaining a more honest sense of who we authentically want to be as a human being and using this to guide how we present ourselves across all aspects of our life. With this in mind, it's time to now apply C–E–P (Contemplate–Express–Practice).

> **SOMETHING TO TRY:**
> Take some time to contemplate the following questions.
> Where you feel comfortable, discuss the concepts with others
> as you build a plan for how you will bring your answers to life.
> At the back of this book is space to capture notes as you dive
> into answering 'Who am I?'
>
> *Level 1: Physical*
> - How do I feel about my physical self, including my health,
>   fitness, appearance and presence, etc?
> - How do I feel about my physical surroundings, including
>   where and how I live, my possessions and tidiness, etc?
> - Is this how I authentically want to feel about these things?
> - How do I want people to perceive me across the physical level?
>
> *To guide your action also answer:*
>
> - What changes will I make to bring to life what I authentically
>   want across the physical level?
>
> *Level 2: Social*
> - How do I feel about my relationships with others?
> - What do those relationships contribute to me and what do
>   I contribute to them?
> - How do I authentically want to feel about my relationship
>   with others?

- How do I want people to experience me in my relationship
  with them?

To guide your action also answer:

- What changes will I make to bring to life what I authentically
  want across the social level?

Level 3: Personal

- How do I feel about being me?
- What do I like about myself?
- What do I dislike about myself?
- How do I authentically want to feel about being me?
- How do I want people to perceive how I feel about myself?

To guide your action also answer:

- What changes will I make to bring to life what I authentically
  want across the personal level?

Level 4: Spiritual

- *How do I feel about what is important to me—that is, am I
  honest with myself about what is really important to me?*
- *Where do I currently focus my attention and energy?*
- *How do I authentically want to feel about what is important to me?*
- *How do I want people to know what is important to me?*

To guide your action also answer:

- What changes will I make to bring to life what I authentically
  want across the spiritual level?

The questions involved in creating an authentic identity are deep and often confronting because they force us to look into the mirror in terms of how we are leading and living our lives. Using these questions, however, helps us to challenge some of the assumptions and beliefs that are holding together the sedimented aspects of our identity. Through the stories of Mike and Lucy below, we realise that by challenging the assumptions and beliefs which underpin our sense of identity, we can be more conscious about how we measure up across each of the four levels. This ultimately helps us to be more comfortable in our own skin through establishing a more authentic identity.

Who am I? Mike's story

Through hard work and being willing to take on the toughest projects, Mike had been promoted rapidly. He'd reached director level and was earning a good salary. In spite of him trying to position himself as the Great Man, Mike felt something was missing. He'd never admitted it to others, but when Mike stopped to think about 'who he was', he recognised that he had inadvertently made many sacrifices across the four levels to achieve what he had.

Physical—Due to the amount of travel he believed he needed to do in his national role, Mike had stopped exercising and had fallen into a habit of eating on the run, rather than being conscious of his diet. His office had become his company car, hotel rooms and the sofa at home, which is where he tried to catch up after his family had gone to bed. Physically, he was tired and out of shape. '*I feel like I'm caught on the hamster wheel, where each day I've just got to survive,'* Mike said during one of our early coaching sessions.

Social—Through Mike's beliefs about how he had to perform his role, he was very rarely home with free time. This not only impacted the time he spent with his immediate family, but it also impacted the time he had to spend with his extended family and friends. Although he was well regarded by all those at work and had strong relationships with his colleagues, Mike felt lonely. '*At work everybody wants time with me,*' Mike stated. '*But outside of work it's like I'm just a bolt-on to a world that exists without me.*'

Personal—With all that he'd sacrificed, when we got to how Mike authentically felt about being himself, he stated '*I resent my life!*' Mike resented the fact that he'd allowed himself to change so much. He resented the fact that it felt like it was easier for him to stay on the 'hamster wheel' rather than make a change. Beyond this, however, what Mike liked about himself was the fact that he was determined and driven. That, if he put his mind to it, he could create positive change in his life.

Spiritual—Due to where he was directing his energy, it seemed clear that work was Mike's highest priority. However, when we explored it further it became very clear that this really wasn't the case. In spite of where he was directing his energy, what was important to Mike was to be respected and to feel as if he was making a difference to those around him inside of work and outside of work. Yes, the big salary was good, but this was only a consequence of progressing in his career, and not something that drove him. Mike's actions were therefore at odds with what was most important to him.

Who am I?—Within Mike's answers to the questions across the four levels there were two beliefs that provide powerful catalysts for change. The first was in relation to how he had to perform his role. Through challenging his assumptions about his role, we were able to give Mike back some of his most valuable resource: time. Mike began travelling less and created more of a routine around his working practice. Through doing this, not only was he able to focus back on his physical self, but he could also use the time to invest in his social self. His relationships became stronger and in service of what was most important to him. How did he achieve this? He relied on his second catalyst for change: his drive and determination. And through this, not only did Mike regain focus and intention in his life but he also became more effective in all the roles he performed in work and outside of work. At the most basic level, Mike's answer to 'Who am I?' went from being a 'busy, resentful professional' to 'I'm Mike, a caring and focused father, husband, son, friend and professional, who is here to make the most positive difference I can.'

Who am I? Lucy's story

Lucy was regarded by many as being naturally talented. She was put up on a pedestal as a 'Great Man'. Almost all the people around her marvelled at her ability to succeed at everything she put her mind to, and as a result was said to 'have it all'. In spite of this apparent perfect existence, Lucy felt like an imposter. She felt as though the image of how she was perceived caused her to be held up as the role model for others to follow. What they missed, however, is that this was not how Lucy felt about herself. '*There's a long way to fall, when they realise that I'm not as good as they think,*' Lucy stated, sharing her fears.

Physical—Due to how she felt people perceived her, Lucy believed that she had to over-invest in her physical level. '*My world has to look perfect,*' she stated during one of the activities in our leadership retreat. '*Whether it's how I look, or where I live, it all has to look perfect,*' she reinforced, '*otherwise people may learn the truth.*' Unfortunately, holding this belief about needing to create a perfect image prevented her from ever relaxing, and just enjoying 'being'.

Social—At the social level, the majority of Lucy's relationships were with people who were also considered to be perfect. Both in work and outside of work, she seemed to have become surrounded by people who were more focused on image than anything else. This left Lucy in a perpetual state of anxiety, where she felt that she was having to live up to the expectations of others rather than showing any level of vulnerability. '*I seem to have lost contact with people who like me for who I am,*' she said.

Personal—Exploring the personal level, it was clear that Lucy did not like who she had become. '*This isn't the real me,*' she stated. '*I'm not this perfect person, I'm just Lucy.*' Through this realisation, and connected to the social level, Lucy committed to wanting to feel good about herself, being more comfortable in her own skin rather than trying to live up to what she perceived others expected of her.

Spiritual—Lucy was clear on what was important to her, especially in terms of her family and her team, although this was not where her energy was invested. Committed to redress this balance, involved her investing less energy in trying to live up to the perceptions of others, and investing more energy in supporting those who mattered most, especially herself.

Who am I?—Within Lucy's answers to the questions across the four levels it was clear that she felt trapped trying to live up to the inflated perceptions of other people rather than trying to find comfort in her own skin. Through being more conscious of how she authentically wanted to feel across the four levels, she was able to let go of the definition of needing to be 'perfect' and instead focus her energy on that which mattered most to her: feeling good about herself and giving the best contribution she could to those around her. Although Lucy didn't fundamentally change any aspect of her life, she made subtle but powerful shifts across each of the four levels. At the physical level, she was kinder to herself about her physical self and surroundings, accepting that how she looked and how she lived didn't need to be 'perfect' every day. At the social level, she prioritised connecting with people who she could help and support as well as reconnecting with people who accepted her for who she was. At a personal level, she let go of her fears of being found out and thus allowed herself to believe in what she was good at, no longer feeling like an imposter. And finally, at a spiritual level, she invested energy in that which mattered most to her, caring less if people didn't perceive her as being perfect. At the most basic level, Lucy's answer to 'Who am I?' went from being 'a perfect façade hiding an imperfect person,' to 'I'm Lucy. I'm good at what I do, and I like who I am.'

QUESTION 2: WHY AM I HERE?

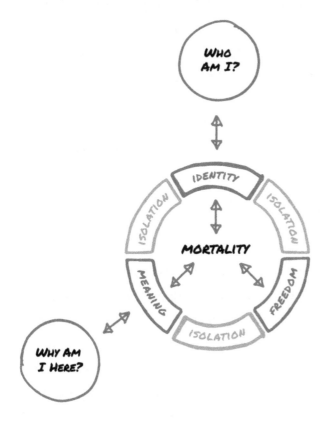

'I'm doing a stand-up show next Saturday night,' Tom told me excitedly as we walked towards the station after a day together on a coaching course.

'That's great,' I replied, disappointed that I'd miss it because my family and I were going to be away.

'It's the only thing that I've always wanted to do, but never have,' he concluded.

At the station we said our goodbyes. As I walked away, I marvelled how, at sixty years old, Tom was still challenging himself to do new things. What I missed in that short conversation, however, was what he was really trying to tell me, because that was the last time that I saw Tom.

A week after his show he took his own life. Why? Because amongst other reasons, at sixty he believed he'd done all that he'd wanted to in life.

The moral of the story: *As Friedrich Nietzsche, the German philosopher, wrote: 'He who has a why to live can bear almost any how'.*

* * *

FROM WHO, TO WHY

With the definition of our authentic identity evolving, we can begin contemplating the second question: 'Why am I here?' It is important to reinforce the fact that without at least contemplating the first question of 'Who am I?' before focusing on 'Why am I here?', we allow the insecurities and hang-ups that often exist within our identity to influence our sense of meaning and purpose. As was highlighted under the human dilemma of meaning, when insecurity plagues our identity, contemplating meaning sees us risk becoming like the beauty pageant contestant stating that we will use our life to bring world peace when this is far removed from what is actually important to us in our day-to-day lives.

WHY = PURPOSE

As meaning-making creatures, we need a reason for why things happen. Contemplating and answering the question 'Why am I here?' therefore helps us embrace the human dilemma of meaning. It helps us discover what is truly important to us, which provides us not only with meaning but also a sense of purpose and direction.

In today's world, where the pressures of the Age of Accelerations are unrelenting, it's easy to be swept along with the tide, especially if you're in a leadership role. As Adam Hochschild, the author, historian and lecturer says, 'Work is hard. Distractions are plentiful. And time is short.' Furthermore, facing a continual flow of often conflicting priorities, it's easy to start sacrificing those things which are actually most important to us as we try to keep our head above the water. And when we do this, we create stories to help justify that it's the right thing to do.

. . .

'We're so busy at the moment. I'm having to put our son into nursery from 8:00 to 18:00 every day,' the manager I was coaching said to me.

'But,' she continued, 'he's got great friends and has a lot of fun there, and then I've got time with him from 18:00 until he goes to bed at 19:30.'

. . .

In any given moment, it is easy to cast judgement on ourselves for how we're spending our time and what this says about what's important to us. The key is to let go of the judgement and be really honest with ourselves about why we are doing what we're doing, and whether this actually satisfies what's most important to us. That is, answering the question: 'Why am I here?'

PARADOX OF PURPOSE

When contemplating 'Why am I here?', we draw our attention to discovering our sense of purpose for this moment and for all moments of our life. The sense of purpose that we create is what gives us meaning. It is why we get out of bed each day.

Having a sense of purpose is deeply personal. It is ours to own and the satisfaction of our purpose is what brings us the success and fulfilment that we're seeking. And this applies whether we are talking about a moment in our day, or all moments of our life. Seeking to satisfy our sense of purpose is therefore deeply selfish; it's something we want to do, so we may achieve success and fulfilment. However, herein lies the paradox: satisfying our sense of purpose can only be done through our contribution to others, especially when we're in a leadership role. Thus, the contribution we make through our purpose is selfless.

$$Purpose = Selfishness \infty Selflessness$$

Recognising the paradox of purpose means that we can be more honest with ourselves about why we do what we do, and we can be more honest about the contribution we are seeking to make each and every moment of our life.

SOURCES OF PURPOSE

When answering 'Why am I here?', creating it in the moment by merely stating that 'my purpose is ...' is not sufficient. Responses like this become transactional and restrictive, and often don't bring the sense of meaning that give us real purpose. For example, 'to pay the mortgage' versus 'to provide a safe and comfortable home for my family'.

Viktor Frankl, an Auschwitz survivor and author of many books including *Man's Search for Meaning*[10], states that to discover our purpose we need to dig deeper. And we do this through looking at the following potential sources:

- **Recurring themes throughout life**—often our desire to contribute something greater than ourselves has 'shown up' throughout our lives in the form of recurring themes of contribution. For example, we may have had a pattern for being drawn to particular causes or behaviours that contribute positively to others.

- **Challenges or adversity**—through overcoming challenges or adversity ourselves we find purpose in helping others to do the same. For example, we may have experienced tragedy in our family or friendship group that provides a cause for us to focus on.

- **Work or deeds we undertake**—recognising that rarely does the work we undertake or deeds we complete focus only on ourselves helps us to look at the contribution we are making to others. For example, we may recognise how the work we do day to day brings meaning to others.

Beyond these, I believe that there is one further source which is directly related to the positive difference we are making to those we care most about. Personally, these people may be our family and friends. Professionally, these people may be our team members or colleagues.

Irrespective of the source of our purpose, it is about the positive contribution we make to those around us.

DISCOVERING PURPOSE

Discovering our purpose through answering 'Why am I here?' is distinct from defining our purpose. The reason for using the word 'discovering' is because it is likely that you are already focused on it, even if unconsciously.

. . .

'So, why do you do this?' I asked the partner from one of the Big Four accounting and professional services firms at the start of our second coaching session.

'When you asked me that in our last session,' he replied, 'I'll admit that I was completely lost. I'd never even contemplated it.'

'But,' he continued, after taking a sip of his tea, 'as I thought about it more, I realised it's about three things. I love watching people grow and develop in my team. I love helping clients solve problems which make their lives easier. And thirdly, by doing those things I love being able to give my family a life full of adventure and fun.'

'It's always three things with you consultants,' I mocked, delighted at his discovery.

. . .

To discover our purpose and hence create an answer for 'Why am I here?', we need to consider some questions:

- **Who are you making a contribution to?**
  This helps us consider those who are the people most important to us, which we feel compelled to help and support in some way. Being clear on who we are making a contribution to ensures that we are also clear on the needs they have.

- **What impact will that contribution have on them?**
  This helps us consider the positive difference we are trying to make to those we are seeking to make a contribution to. Being clear on the impact ensures that the contribution we make actually satisfies the needs of those people.

- **How will you make that contribution?**
  This helps us consider the way in which we will make the positive difference. Being clear on how we will make the contribution ensures that we have planned how we will invest our time and energy and how we will make the required resources available.

- **What does that contribution give you?**
  This helps us consider what needs within us we are trying to satisfy. Being clear on what making the contribution gives us personally helps us make sure that we are also satisfying our own needs.

Through these questions we focus not only on what the contribution is and how we make it, but we also embrace the paradox of purpose by recognising what impact it has on others (selflessness), and what benefit making that impact gives us (selfishness).

OVER TO YOU ...

Answering the question of 'Why am I here?' isn't about establishing some grand life purpose that you tell others whenever asked 'What do you do?'; that's Great Man thinking. It is about being honest with yourself about what's most important to you and consciously discovering a sense of purpose that is both selfish in terms of helping you achieve the success and fulfilment you desire, and selfless in terms of making a positive contribution to others. With this in mind, it's time to now apply C–E–P (Contemplate–Express–Practice).

> **SOMETHING TO TRY:**
> Take some time to contemplate the following questions. Where you feel comfortable, discuss the concepts with others as you build a plan for how you will bring your answers to life. At the back of this book is space to capture notes as you consider the responses to these questions.
>
> - *Who are you making a contribution to?*
> - *What impact will that contribution have on them?*
> - *How will you make that contribution? Be specific.*
> - *What does making that contribution give you?*

> Where there is more than one party that you're making a contribution to, capture each party separately.

The questions involved in defining the contribution you are seeking to make in answering 'Why am I here?' are powerful. Through the stories of Georgia and Tony we realise that to lead and live with greater purpose doesn't mean that we need to change the entire world. It does, however, mean that we start to make a more positive contribution to the lives of those we care about, which ultimately gives us a greater sense of success and fulfilment.

Why am I here? Georgia's story

'*I don't feel like I have a purpose,*' Georgia admitted, as we discussed what she felt was missing from her life. '*I get up, get the children ready for school, drop them off, go to work, pick the children up, cook them dinner, eventually put them to bed and then slump on the sofa before also going to bed.*' From her admission, Georgia described herself being in a rut. Although Georgia had positioned herself as the Great Man by ensuring all those around her were dependent on her, she felt like she was existing each day without a deeper sense of purpose. Beyond the routine of everyday life, Georgia didn't feel like she was contributing anything. '*There's more I can give,*' Georgia stated, revealing her desire for a different path.

Through exploring the questions associated with 'Why am I here?', it became clear that Georgia was very passionate about a range of issues where she felt like she could make a greater difference. In particular, based on the recurring theme of support she had through her life, she identified that she wanted to 'pay it forward', as she called it, by giving the same level of support to others. Responding to this desire, and after further exploration and planning, within her organisation Georgia created mentor and support groups for colleagues wanting to learn about new topics. She also extended this concept into the local community, partnering with charities so she could support those less fortunate than herself.

The sense of purpose she gained through this contribution gave her new focus and energy, which flowed into her day-to-day life. This caused Georgia to stop viewing each day as a routine that had to be followed. She now saw each day as an opportunity to make a more positive difference to the lives of everyone with whom she came into contact. At the most basic level, Georgia's answer to 'Why am I here?' went from being 'to make it through each day', to 'I'm Georgia, my purpose is to help those I meet make the best of the opportunities available to them.'

Why am I here? Tony's story

As a finance director, Tony had followed a very classic career path. Starting as a graduate auditor in a large accountancy firm, he then eventually joined a finance team in a company and worked his way up to the top. As the finance director, Tony's day job was busy. Caught trying to sustain the Great Man image that came with the title, often his day would consist of back-to-back meetings where he would have little time to go to the bathroom, let alone make a bigger contribution. *'There's got to be more to life than this*,' Tony admitted, as he shared his frustration with his current way of being.

After challenging many of the beliefs regarding how Tony performed his role through the questions associated with 'Who am I?', Tony gained head space (time and energy) to focus on the questions relating to 'Why am I here?'. Very quickly Tony's desire for greater meaning and purpose in his life became apparent. In seeking to define the contribution he felt he had to offer, Tony kept coming back to the work he did. '*I'm really good with managing finances*,' he said, '*that's my superpower*.' Through this realisation, Tony focused on who he could help through his 'superpower'. Those he chose to make a stronger contribution to initially included his direct team, who through his busyness had felt disempowered. He spent more time coaching and developing his team resulting in their confidence and capability improving, allowing them to add even greater value to the organisation. Supported by his team, Tony then expanded his influence into the broader organisation, helping those across the business better understand how to manage finance and thus increase the value they also delivered in the business. Unexpectedly for Tony, the impact of this went beyond the business also. '*Someone came up to me yesterday and told me that the session we ran on managing budgets not only helped them in their role, but also at home*,' Tony explained, feeling energised by the impact he and his team were having.

As Tony's team took on greater responsibility, he was given more time to focus on making a contribution to others. The sense of purpose Tony gained helped him be even more effective in his day job and opened up other opportunities, including non-executive roles. At the most basic level, Tony's answer to 'Why am I here?' went from being 'to be the finance director of our company', to 'I'm Tony, my purpose is to enable others to deliver the greatest value they can.'

QUESTION 3: HOW WILL I LEAD AND LIVE?

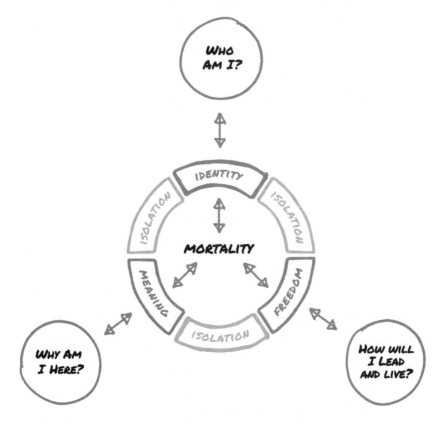

'It's odd,' the senior director said to me as we both sat down.

'What is?' I asked.

'Well,' she continued, 'since I've been working on answering the first of the two questions, strange things have happened.'

'What sort of strange things?' I asked, feeling curious.

'Just different things,' she said. 'I've found myself in conversations where there's been new opportunities both in work and outside of work.'

She paused to collect her thoughts.

'It's as if,' she continued, 'answering "Who am I?" and "Why am I here?" has opened up a new world to me.'

'I guess when our consciousness shifts we pay attention to different things,' I responded, realising that we were now ready to focus on the third question.

The moral of the story: *Where our mind goes, our energy flows.*

• • •

OPENING TO OPPORTUNITY

Through answering 'Who am I?', our definition of our authentic identity begins to evolve. This creates a foundation for answering 'Why am I here?', which helps us discover our sense of purpose in terms of what is most important to us. As we deepen our understanding of our answers to these questions, our attention shifts. No longer are we living in the shadow of the Great Man, unnecessarily consuming energy on insecurities and hang-ups about who we are and how people perceive us. And no longer are we consuming energy on that which isn't important to us. This means we have even greater head space to notice and be open to opportunity; we allow synchronicity to happen.

Carl Jung, the famous Swiss psychologist, described synchronicity as 'a meaningful coincidence of two or more events, where something other than the probability of chance is involved'[11]. As an example, after both taking time off work one afternoon, my wife and I went to a local bar for a drink. She had decided to leave her job and was looking for a new one. As she went to the bathroom, I picked up my phone to check my email. The first email was from a recruitment consultant contact who wanted to know if I'd be interested in a new job, or if I wasn't, if I knew anybody who was. My reply, after talking to my wife, was that I had someone in mind! After five weeks thinking about it, that was the job my wife ended up choosing. Now I get many emails like that each month and so there's nothing significant about it. However, in that moment my wife and I were talking about her future, and so that email became instantly meaningful. Synchronicity happened!

When we step onto the new path for our leadership, our consciousness and attention shifts. This means we pay attention to different things and we become aware of different opportunities. To build momentum as we continue asking and answering 'Who am I?' and 'Why am I here?', we must focus on directing our attention and energy in a more mindful way. To do this requires answering the third question, 'How will I lead and live?'

LEADING **AND** LIVING

In answering the first two questions it is nearly impossible to separate work from life. Why? Because this is an artificial dualism. And because, whether we like it or not, we are a single, isolated human being who doesn't leave what happens outside of work at home each morning, and we don't leave what happens inside work at the office each night. We are human beings who have an identity and sense of purpose. And whilst these may flex and adapt to circumstances, to remain authentic, the core of who we are and why we're here doesn't change even if the behaviour we adopt to bring them to life does. Recognising this means that, as we seek to answer the third question, our focus has to be on how we lead and live. Where the act of leading and living is something that we do, both inside and outside work.

ACTING WITH MINDFUL INTENTION

Answering 'How will I lead and live?' helps us embrace our human dilemma of freedom. It helps us recognise that we have an inescapable responsibility to choose, where electing to not choose is still making a choice.

To help us embrace the dilemma of freedom, answering 'How will I lead and live?' causes us to act with mindful intention. That is, no longer do we find clever ways to avoid or abdicate our responsibility for our freedom. Instead, we mindfully embrace it, consciously owning our choices and being clear on how we will act. And through being mindful, we recognise that very few decisions are fully irreversible, which helps us to then take a more experimental approach. That is, we recognise that each decision creates a new path with new possibilities.

CALIBRATING OUR AUTOPILOT

As stated earlier in this book, the human brain is the most energy-consuming organ in the body. This is why we can still feel exhausted after an intensive day-long meeting even though we've barely left our seat. As also stated, to help remain efficient and conserve energy, as a species we've learned to make instinctive as many routine tasks as possible. For example, how much thought do you give to brushing your teeth each day? So for the vast majority of our day, we effectively operate on autopilot.

As humans we're not able to completely switch off autopilot. We have neither the mental capacity nor capability to do this. And the truth is, we wouldn't really want to. Would you want to consciously think about every single task you perform, every single day?

To act with mindful intention, and hence answer 'How will I lead and live?', we therefore need to do two things. Firstly, we need to recognise when our autopilot isn't helping us. And secondly, in those areas where our autopilot is getting in the way of our success and fulfilment, we need to recalibrate it by building the right habits.

BUILDING THE RIGHT HABITS

'We are what we repeatedly do. Excellence, therefore, is not an act, but a habit.'

Aristotle

Habits are effectively the way our autopilot works. Over time, as we learn new things that serve us, they get formed into a habit. And, because our habits are so well entrenched, most of them are unconscious.

With our answers to both 'Who am I?' and 'Why am I here?' evolving, focusing on 'How will I lead and live?' gives us the opportunity to conduct an audit of our habits. Starting with our definition of our authentic identity, 'Who am I?', we can explore what habits we currently have that support or inhibit our responses across the four levels. We can also identify those new habits which we need to create. For example, if in the physical world our authentic desire is to be fit and healthy, then a habit of eating too much fast food isn't going to be useful. In this case we may want to remove this fast-food habit and replace it with a habit of eating healthier meals and reducing snacks.

Moving to 'Why am I here?', again we can audit the habits that support or inhibit satisfying our sense of purpose, and we can create new habits to help us. For example, if one aspect of our contribution is to spend quality time with our family, then a habit of taking our work devices on holiday is not going to serve that purpose. In this case we may either want to not take our devices on holiday, or we may seek to be really disciplined about when we check them, so we spend the quality time we desire with those we love.

When auditing our habits, the key is to be clear in assessing how our habits support or inhibit the fulfilment of our identity and purpose, and what new habits might need to be formed to replace those which don't help us. Through building the right habits we calibrate our autopilot enabling us to lead and live with greater mindful intention. For example, a previous manager I knew found herself consistently feeling tense each evening when she picked her children up from nursery. Counter to her authentic identity of wanting to be a great mum who gave her children the attention and love they needed, this resulted in her having very little patience for them even though they were excited to see her. When exploring the habits that existed around this event it seemed that she would always check her work email on the walk from the train station to the nursery. Doing this, however, caused her to carry into the nursery the pressure of what was in her inbox. Simply changing this habit so she no longer checked her email before walking into the nursery was transformational. 'I now give my children my full attention rather than feeling like they're just another thing to attend to,' she described, feeling like she was now better fulfilling her identity and purpose as a mother.

MANAGE ENERGY, NOT TIME

Beyond habits, to recalibrate our autopilot we must also recognise that our energy levels fluctuate through each day and each week. Relating to circadian rhythms*, the energy cycle of each person will be different. For me, I'm freshest and most energised first thing in the morning, especially if I've exercised. For others I've worked with, it's not until lunchtime before their energy levels hit peak. Rather than use this knowledge to our advantage, however, classically what we do is just see the day as blocks of time. Our diaries rule our lives, trapping us in the illusion that in each block of time we are equally effective.

Recognising how our level of energy fluctuates through the day helps us manage our energy better rather than our time. That is, if there are certain tasks that require deep thought, then they should be done at a time when we are most energised. This means we use a 'block of time' when we have the right level of energy to perform

---

* Circadian rhythms relate to how our biological clock regulates the functions of our body. Our circadian rhythms influence our effectiveness throughout the day, influencing how much energy we have, based on the release of different neurochemicals into the body. For example, when it's time to wake up, the body starts releasing cortisol, and when it is time to go to sleep, the body starts releasing melatonin.

the task. Leaving the task to a time when we don't have the right level of energy will make the task feel more laborious than it is. For example, I know I have more energy in the morning and this is when I am able to concentrate most effectively. The morning is therefore when I schedule to do complex tasks, like preparing proposals or reviewing contracts. Leaving these tasks to later in the day always causes me to take longer and I have to concentrate harder.

When we more consciously manage our energy not only does it help us lead and live with greater mindful intention, but we are also more effective in the things we do.

ELIMINATING DISTRACTIONS

As humans we're prone to distraction. This comes from our early evolution where the number of mortal threats in our environment were far greater, so being constantly alert was essential for our survival. In spite of the number of mortal threats declining, being prone to distraction has remained part of our make-up. In response to this, some people claim that they are excellent multitaskers. However, as many of us will know from our own lives, multitasking only reduces our ability to get things done rather than enhancing it. Clifford Nass, professor of psychology at Stanford University, reinforces this, stating that 'the research is almost unanimous, which is very rare in social science, and it says that people who chronically multitask show an enormous range of deficits. They're basically terrible at all sorts of cognitive tasks, including multitasking'[12].

To help us remain focused, as we seek to lead and live with greater mindful intention it is critical to eliminate distractions.

However, with the intrusive nature of our technology, the sources of distraction are numerous. Each of our smart devices has been designed to steal and hold all our attention throughout our every waking hours. To manage distractions, there are many things that can be done to help us, such as turning off notifications and putting devices onto flight mode for periods of the day. Deciding what to do, however, starts with recognising when we become distracted and then having the discipline to do something about it.

OVER TO YOU ...

With our evolving definition of 'Who am I?' and discovery of 'Why am I here?', we shift our attention. This helps us direct our energy and where we spend our time better. Answering 'How will I lead and live?' completes the circle of 'The 3 Questions'™ by bringing intention to our actions. That is, through 'The 3 Questions'™ we start to lead and live with greater 'mindful' intention. To take first steps in showing leadership, we must therefore recognise what we do that helps and hinders us. This starts with conducting an audit of our habits against our answers to the first two questions. It then involves being clear about how we manage our energy and eliminating our distractions.

It should be noted that the concept of establishing habits, managing energy and eliminating distractions might appear tactical in the face of a deeper set of questions. However, without attention at this level it is difficult to maintain the focus as the pressures of day-to-day life impact us. With this in mind, it's time to now apply C–E–P (Contemplate–Express–Practice).

SOMETHING TO TRY:

Take some time to contemplate the following questions. Where you feel comfortable, discuss the concepts with others as you build a plan for how you will bring your answers to life. At the back of this book is space to capture notes as you consider the responses to these questions.

Against what you've captured for 'Who am I?' and Why am I here?', identify:

- What current habits help or get in the way of you bringing to life your authentic identity and sense of purpose? In identifying these consider what habits do you need to let go of and what further habits do you need to establish?
- What is your usual energy cycle through the day and week? When are you at your most and least energised and effective? What can you do to better manage your energy rather than your time?
- What distractions most heavily affect you? What can you do to eliminate these distractions?

The questions involved in defining how we will lead and live with mindful intention force us to consider how we focus our energy and spend our time each day. Through the continued stories of Mike, Lucy, Georgia and Tony we see that the changes they make in their lives through the third of 'The 3 Questions'™, although appear simple, were immensely powerful for them.

How will I lead and live? Mike's story

Prior to answering the first of 'The 3 Questions'™, Mike had trapped himself in a set of beliefs about how he had to live his life and perform his role. '*But as a senior leader, you have to be busier than your team,*' he said at one point in our conversation. '*In a national role I have to be on the road every day each week,*' he justified to himself. It was assumptions like these which influenced the habits that defined how he lived his life. And against the question of 'Who am I?' these habits were primarily impacting his physical and social levels, resulting in a loss of health and fitness and a loss social connection. '*I feel like I'm a bolt-on to my family and friends,*' is how he described his social situation.

Letting go of the false promises of being the Great Man, through the questions associated with 'How will I lead and live?', Mike created a new set of habits based on a deeper understanding of the patterns in his energy levels and what distracted him. Mike realised he was fresher and more able to think clearly at the start of the week and so set this time aside for more intellectually challenging work. He created a new routine for meeting with his direct reports and broader team, relying more heavily on using technology rather than travelling. This gave him more time in the day without loss of connection with his team. He established a new routine of exercise every morning, which also gave him more energy through the day. He consciously set time to be with his family for dinner, to take his children to their sports games and he made sure he had time to catch up with friends.

Through starting with establishing habits over the course of each week and each month, Mike tested what worked and what didn't and then embedded what worked as a new set of behaviours. Mike started leading and living with more mindful intention.

How will I lead and live? Lucy's story

Caught trying to live up to the Great Man expectations that were seemingly thrust onto her by others, Lucy felt overwhelmed by needing to be 'perfect' in the eyes of others. In the midst of the paradox of self-awareness, where she was over-regulating her behaviour, Lucy had never stopped to define who she authentically wanted to be. Through creating this definition using the question of 'Who am I?', Lucy then set about challenging her existing habits in terms of how they were supporting or inhibiting her. In doing this, one key area of focus for Lucy was managing her relationships with those people around her. She became conscious of who energised her, helping her feel good about herself and who helped her make a more positive contribution, and those who de-energised her. In recognising this, she sought to manage these relationships proactively. '*I now give more time to the people and areas of my life which give me energy,*' she explained. '*Before, to ensure people saw me as "perfect" I would just give everything I could to everyone,*' she continued. '*But this left me exhausted, because some people are just energy vampires, where you can never give them enough.*'

Through shifting the nature of her relationships in support of her definition of her authentic identity, Lucy learned to say 'no' a lot more. She also learned to manage her relationships in a way that worked for her, giving her more energy to invest in both herself and the positive contribution she could make to others.

How will I lead and live? Georgia's story

Through answering the first two of 'The 3 Questions'™, Georgia realised she was holding onto the need to be in control as the Great Man. As a result, Georgia was firmly running on autopilot each day and unconsciously following a routine without ever challenging whether the routine was helping her unlock her potential or the potential of those around her. She also learned that she had a deep desire to 'pay it forward' in terms of helping people make the most of opportunities available to them. In recognising this, Georgia '*woke up*', as she described it, to the fact that she was just leading and living on autopilot. '*I'd stopped questioning how I was spending my time each day,*' Georgia said. '*It's as if I was just doing the same things day in and day out, never considering whether they were the best things for me to be doing.*' Georgia's further admission related to her continual state of distraction. '*It was easier to be distracted than face some of the questions I should have been asking,*' she said. '*I would actually look for things to fill my day almost as if to avoid having to deal with the frustrations I had about my life.*'

Georgia's realisation that she was leading and living on autopilot proved to be a powerful catalyst in support of her learning to lead and live with greater mindful intention. Through her realisation and recognising where she had the most energy each day, she focused on changing her routine. This was both in changing her home routine and also her work routine. '*I think my children found it a shock at first,*' she described. '*They are now a lot more responsible for themselves rather than me feeling like I'm their servant.*' At work, Georgia also took control of her diary, especially in managing the range of distractions that impacted her. '*I was being pulled in so many different directions, just because I said yes to everything,*' she said. Changing this involved being more discerning about what she got involved with and what she didn't. It also involved using her desire to help people make the most out of opportunities to give greater responsibility to her team.

Through changing her routines and being more conscious of the type of distractions that she was opening herself up to, Georgia gave herself the headspace to focus on her contribution to those around her. This ultimately gave her a stronger sense of purpose which further contributed to the development of her authentic sense of identity.

How will I lead and live? Tony's story

Having developed in the finance function in the same company through his career, Tony was very comfortable. He was very highly respected and seen as doing a great job. Although he was very busy each day, intellectually he was coasting. Deep down, Tony felt like he wanted to do more but was struggling with the time to initially even consider what 'more' would involve.

Through answering the first two of 'The 3 Questions'™, Tony realised that he'd created an environment where he was the Great Man within the team. He had unconsciously positioned himself as the all-seeing, all-knowing leader that everyone went to for answers. In realising this, Tony also acknowledged that he was '*the single point of failure that was holding others back*', as he described it. Changing the habitual patterns of behaviour that underpinned his status started with simply asking questions rather than giving answers. '*It was unsettling for the team at first,*' Tony said, describing their reaction. However, very quickly Tony's team adapted to his new approach and then new ideas on how they should do things started flowing in. '*Not only did I get time back,*' Tony explained, '*but we also started improving how we did things. It was if the flood gates opened.*' By changing his habits, building on Tony's new-found skill of asking questions along with using his 'superpower' of finance resulted in him finding new ways to help unlock the potential of others.

Through changing his habitual patterns of behaviour, Tony let go of needing to be the Great Man. '*It was uncomfortable at first,*' he said, '*but I found my value was not in trying to be the smartest guy in the room. My value was helping others realise the value they had to offer.*'

'THE 3 QUESTIONS'™ = SHOWING LEADERSHIP

Through 'The 3 Questions'™ we create our own path to start showing leadership. To show leadership is to achieve the success and fulfilment we're seeking whilst making a more positive contribution to all those around us. To show leadership is to live and lead with greater authenticity, purpose and mindful intention.

CREATING A VIRTUOUS CYCLE

Through contemplating and answering 'The 3 Questions'™ we establish a different, more personal, human definition for how we show leadership. And although presented sequentially starting with 'Who am I?', through 'The 3 Questions'™ we create a virtuous cycle where our identity, purpose and practice for showing leadership develop over time. 'The 3 Questions'™ therefore help us to confront the uncertainty created by the Age of Accelerations, and equip us to embrace the vulnerability in ourselves created by the human dilemmas in a healthier way. In doing this, the virtuous cycle continues as our identity, purpose and practice for showing leadership evolves through a never-ending process of contemplation and development. That is, 'The 3 Questions'™ are not something we answer once and for all. They are the foundation for how we lead and live across all aspects of our life into the future.

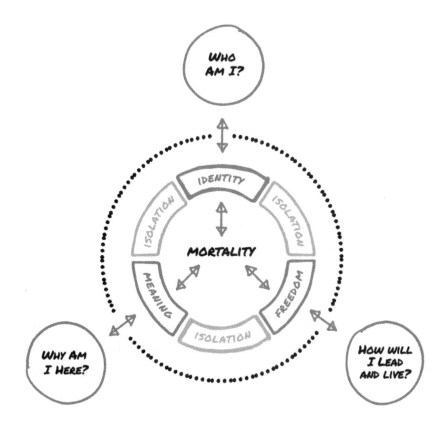

SHOWING LEADERSHIP IS A MINDFUL PRACTICE

In 2010, I was asked to attend an executive assessment programme for the company that employed me. Over three days, my colleagues and I were going to be assessed to determine whether we had the potential to reach a more senior level in the company. During one of the many interviews I was asked about how I manage teams.

'I try to spend as much time as I can learning about every individual,' I answered.

'I then try to ensure we work together to set clear objectives and agree how we're going to deliver them,' I continued.

'Rob,' my assessor cut in over the top of me, 'you keep saying "try". Why do you need to "try", why don't you just "do"?'

Pausing for a moment, I looked at the Great Man leader sitting in front of me.

'Well,' I replied with certainty, 'because I never want to assume that I'm good at it.'

The assessor stared at me. A look of disdain appeared on her face.

'I believe,' I continued feeling resolute, 'that when I'm in a leadership role I should always be trying to give my best. I owe that to my team, to the company, and to myself. That's why I say "try"!'

* * *

Through 'The 3 Questions'™ and the definition for our leadership that we establish, we finally let go of our perception that we need to be the Great Man. We no longer feel the need to be the all-seeing, all-knowing, powerful, heroic character who is able to provide certainty. We accept that we are human beings, leading other human beings. And in doing this, we accept that as humans we are magnificent, vulnerable creatures who are not perfect.

By letting go of the need to be the Great Man and acknowledging that we're not perfect, we allow ourselves to show leadership as a mindful practice. Much like any form of mindfulness, showing leadership as a mindful practice acknowledges that we will not get it right all the time, especially in the Age of Accelerations. We will make mistakes. There will be things that surprise us. We will drift from our path. But as a mindful practice we will recognise when we are drifting. We will be kind to ourselves about this. And then, we will seek to bring ourselves back to the path of leading and living with authenticity, purpose and mindful intention. To start showing leadership is therefore to recognise that it is as much about the journey and path we follow as it is about the destination and the contribution we make.

STEPP
INTO T
LIGHT

ING
HE

The Great Man is dead. It's time to show leadership!

In the Age of Accelerations the pace and complexity of change and level of uncertainty is only going to increase. Facing this, the pressure and expectation placed on those in leadership roles will also increase as they seek to confront the experience of anxiety that prevails. With the Great Man no longer being the all-seeing, all-knowing, powerful, heroic character who is able to provide certainty, we find ourselves needing to step into the light in search of our true human potential. To unlock our potential, and the potential of others, we are given two statements:

Stop being a leader

Start showing leadership

Through the statement of 'Stop being a leader', and the 'One Rule' that brings this to life, we're empowered to let go of the classic definitions of leadership that have overshadowed us throughout our lives. In letting go, we recognise that the Great Man model is dead because it no longer helps us achieve the success and fulfilment we're seeking.

With the head space created by applying the 'One Rule' we are afforded time and energy to apply the second statement of 'Start showing leadership'. And we do this through contemplating and answering the 'The 3 Questions'™. Answering 'Who am I?', 'Why am I here?' and 'How will I live and lead?' enables us to create a new path for our leadership. We learn to lead and live with greater authenticity, purpose and mindful intention.

On the surface, applying the One Rule and 'The 3 Questions'™ may seem simple, and in one respect it is. However, what this new philosophy for leadership really expects is that we embrace what it means to be human, and in doing so we follow the guidance of Maharishi Mahesh Yogi, who says:

> *'The important thing is this: to be able, at any moment, to sacrifice what we are for what we could become.'*

To show leadership by applying the One Rule and 'The 3 Questions'™ is therefore a process of continual becoming. And through this 'becoming' we recognise that it is our choice about what we hold on to and what we let go of as we define how we appear to others and where we focus our time and attention. We also recognise that the journey we are on is as important as the destination, and therefore we should learn to enjoy it.

OVER TO YOU ...

The final task in this book is now for you to capture a simple story that defines how you will show leadership across every aspect of your life. At the back of this book is space to capture notes as you consider the responses to these questions.

Take a minute now to capture your story using these three simple statements:

- I am …
- Why I'm here is …
- How I will lead and live is …

In creating your story, the final thing to remember is this: as we've learned from the stories of Mike, Lucy, Georgia and Tony, showing leadership is not about radically changing every aspect of your life. It is about using the 'One Rule' and 'The 3 Questions'™ to help you create your path for leading and living with greater authenticity, purpose and mindful intention so you can achieve the success and fulfilment you are seeking.

A LAST T
— MY U
LESSON
LEADER

HOUGHT

TIMATE

IN

SHIP

'We are always getting ready to live but never living'.

Ralph Waldo Emerson

Looking back over my life, I realise that even before crafting this philosophy I've always been applying the 'One Rule' and 'The 3 Questions'™. I also realise that my answers for 'Who am I?', 'Why am I here?' and 'How will I lead and live?' have evolved to make up the fabric of how I have shown leadership in every aspect of my life.

In the year 2000, after I completed my officer training in the Air Force, I was posted to the Air Force's operational command headquarters. Each day I would sit in a small four-desk cubicle and complete tedious and seemingly pointless tasks, which caused my confidence to gradually erode. Sitting with me and one of my other junior officer colleagues was a Squadron Leader named Dennis. Dennis was approaching retirement after serving in the Air Force his entire career. In spite of the perception I held about the environment we worked in, each morning Dennis would bounce into the office. 'Morning, sir,' I would say before asking how he was. 'I'm excellent thank you Rob,' Dennis would always respond.

Confused by his continual positivity, one day I asked Dennis why he felt so excellent each morning.

'I've been to the slums of Calcutta, Rob,' he responded without hesitation as a blank expression appeared on my face. 'I've got a roof over my head and food in my stomach, so life has to be excellent.'

Beyond this powerful lesson in leadership, Dennis taught me one more thing that stuck with me throughout my life. Whilst working on a project together I was struck by his courage and humility. Whether it was due to his age and experience, or due to the fact that he was about to retire, Dennis had this unique way of challenging the status quo, causing people to reflect on themselves and the impact they were having.

'What do you want to be remembered for?' I asked Dennis as we sat together for lunch one day.

Dennis looked at me and smiled.

'Rob, I don't need to be remembered,' he stated unequivocally. 'I don't care if people end up saying "Dennis, Dennis who?" because this isn't about me.'

Staring at Dennis, I waited for him to continue.

'Rob, too many people are focused only on themselves which gets in the way of them doing their best. All I want to do is make a difference to all the people I meet and to make sure they have what they need to be the best humans they can. And, I don't care whether they recognise that it was me that helped them or not.'

Through my journey that followed the short time I worked with Dennis and the lessons he shared, I have found myself feeling humbled many times. Although, like my fellow humans, I have grappled with my own ego and the pressure of feeling like I need to be the Great Man, I have tried as best I can to appreciate what

I have, especially the preciousness of time. And I have tried to do things for the right reason rather than for self-promotion.

Fast-forwarding to 2018, as I left my last corporate role with a company called SIG Plc, amongst many humbling messages of thanks, I was given one of the most wonderful compliments I believe you can receive: two members of the team I managed thanked me for 'believing in them'. In that moment I couldn't understand why they would say that because it was me who wanted to thank them for all they had taught me.

From all I have learned in my life, especially in working with people in leadership roles over the last twenty years, I recognise that showing leadership is not about being remembered as the Great Man. It is about the contribution we make to others. It is about how through leading and living with greater authenticity, purpose and mindful intention, we not only unlock our own human potential, but we also unlock the potential of those around us, which after all, is what leadership is really all about. And in the Age of Accelerations it is the ability to unlock human potential that is more important than ever before!

It's now over to you to stop being a leader so you can start showing leadership!

It's now over to you to apply the 'One Rule' and 'The 3 Questions'™.

MORE ABOUT ROB CROSS AND MURU LEADERSHIP

Rob Cross is founder and CEO of Muru, a next-generation leadership coaching and development consultancy that debunks the redundant models of what it means to be a leader, to help individuals, teams and groups unlock their true potential.

Born in the United Kingdom and raised in a small country town in Victoria, Australia, Rob's passion for understanding people and leadership started at an early age. After leaving the Air Force in 2004, where he started his career as a civil engineer, Rob returned to the United Kingdom to work for a number of blue-chip companies, including BT, SIG, LexisNexis and the Prudential, leading organisational change and leadership and talent development programmes.

Through his work and in all aspects of life, Rob is recognised as a passionate and inspiring commercially focused speaker, coach, facilitator and executive business leader. His broad international experience across a range of sectors, mixed with his clear focus on practically applying unique, grounded solutions has seen him create real value for organisations and individuals.

Bringing together twenty years of hands-on leadership, and practical experience of developing others, Rob researched, designed and launched Muru Leadership and 'The 3 Questions'™, an innovative new leadership model that unlocks true human potential. In today's Age of Accelerations, where the classic definitions of being a leader are no longer working, 'The 3 Questions'™ methodology helps individuals and teams build greater courage and conviction in their own leadership, empowering them to lead and achieve higher levels of success and fulfilment, both at work and in life.

To learn more about Muru Leadership and 'The 3 Questions'™ and to access useful resources, visit muruleadership.com.

BIBLIOGRAPHY

Becker, E. (1973). *The Denial of Death*. London: Souvenir Press.

Berardi, F. (2009). *The soul at work: From alienation to autonomy.* South Pasadena: Semiotext(e).

Cederstrom, C. and Fleming, P. (2012). *Dead man working.* Alresford: Zero Books.

Clear, J. (2018). *Atomic Habits: An Easy and Proven Way to Make Good Habits and Break Bad Ones.* New York: Random House.

de Berker, A.O., Rutledge, R.B., Mathys, C., Marshall, L., Cross, G.F., Dolan, R.J. and Bestmann, S. (2016). *Computations of Uncertainty Mediate Acute Stress Response in Humans.* Nature Communications: Article 10996.

Frankl, V.E. (2006). *Man's search for Meaning.* Boston: Beacon Press.

Friedman, T.L. (2006). *Thank You for Being Late: An Optimist's Guide to Thriving in the Age of Accelerations.* New York: Penguin Books.

Fry, H. (2018). *Hello World: How to be Human in the Age of the Machine.* London: Penguin Books.

Fukuyama, F. (2018). *Identity: Contemporary Identity Politics and the Struggle for Recognition.* London: Profile Books.

Goffee, R. and Jones, G. (2006). *Why Should Anyone be Led by You? What It Takes to be an Authentic Leader.* Cambridge: Harvard Business School Press.

Haidt, J. (2012). *The Righteous Mind: Why Good People are Divided by Politics and Religion.* London: Penguin Books.

Heidegger, M. (1962). *Being and Time*. Oxford: Blackwell Publishing.

Jung, C.G. (1958). *The Undiscovered Self.* Abingdon: Routledge.

Jung, C.G. (1960). 'Synchronicity: An acausal connecting principle', *The Structure and Dynamics of the Psyche,* Vol. 8 of *The Collected Works of C.G. Jung,* trans. R.F.C Hull. Princeton: Princeton University Press.

Lawler, J. (2005). *The Essence of Leadership? Existentialism and Leadership*. London: Sage Publications.

May, R. (1977). *The Meaning of Anxiety*. New York: Norton.

McAlloon. P. (2003). *I Trawl the Megahertz*. Liberty: EMI Records.

O'Connell, M. (2017). *To be a Machine: Adventures Among Cyborgs, Utopians, Hackers, and the Futurist Solving the Modest Problem of Death*. London: Granta Publications.

Peters, S. (2012). *The Chimp Paradox: The Mind Management Programme for Confidence, Success and Happiness*. London: Random House.

Puett, M. and Gross-Loch, C. (2016). *The Path: A New Way to Think About Everything*. London: Penguin Books.

Rinpoche, S. (2008). *The Tibetan Book of Living and Dying*. San Francisco: Random House.

Rock, D. (2009). *Your brain at Work: Strategies for Overcoming Distraction, Regaining Focus, and Working Smarter All Day Long*. New York: Harper Collins.

Sapolsky, R. (2017). *Behave: The Biology of Humans at Our Best and Worst*. London: Penguin Books.

Spinelli, E. (2015). *Practicing Existential Therapy: The Relational World*. London: Sage Publications.

Storr, W. (2017). *Selfie: How the West Became Self-obsessed*. London: Picador.

Tillich, P. (2014). *The Courage to Be*. London: Yale University Press.

van Deurzen, E. and Hanaway, M. (2012). *Existential Perspectives on Coaching*. Basingstoke: Palgrave Macmillan.

Whyte, D. (2001). *Crossing the Unknown Sea: Work as a Pilgrimage of Identity*. New York: Riverhead Books.

Yalom, I.D. (1980). *Existential Psychotherapy*. New York: Basic Books.

CAPTURE YOUR ANSWERS
TO 'THE 3 QUESTIONS'™

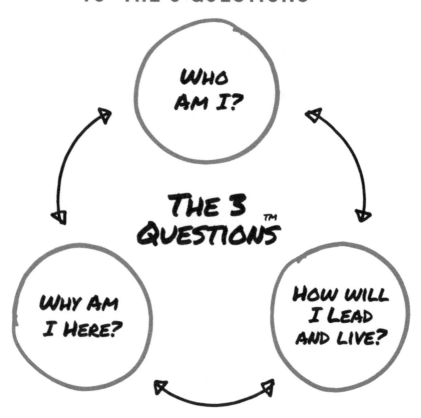

WHO AM I?

Answering the question of 'Who am I?' involves exploring who we authentically want to be across four levels. Use the questions below to guide you.

Level 1: Physical

- How do I feel about my physical self, including my health, fitness, appearance and presence, etc?
- How do I feel about my physical surroundings, including where and how I live, my possessions and tidiness, etc?
- Is this how I authentically want to feel about these things?
- How do I want people to perceive me across the physical level?

To guide your action also answer:

- What changes will I make to bring to life what I authentically want across the physical level?

Level 2: Social

- How do I feel about my relationships with others?
- What do those relationships contribute to me and what do I contribute to them?
- How do I authentically want to feel about my relationship with others?
- How do I want people to experience me in my relationship with them?

To guide your action also answer:

- What changes will I make to bring to life what I authentically want across the social level?

Level 3: Personal

- How do I feel about being me?
- What do I like about myself?
- What do I dislike about myself?
- How do I authentically want to feel about being me?
- How do I want people to perceive how I feel about myself?

To guide your action also answer:

- What changes will I make to bring to life what I authentically want across the personal level?

Level 4: Spiritual

- How do I feel about what is important to me—that is, am I honest with myself about what is really important to me?
- Where do I focus my attention and energy?
- How do I authentically want to feel about what is important to me?
- How do I want people to know what is important to me?

To guide your action also answer:

- What changes will I make to bring to life what I authentically want across the spiritual level?

WHO AM I?

_____

_____

_____

_____

_____

_____

_____

_____

_____

_____

_____

_____

_____

_____

_____

_____

_____

_____

WHO AM I?

_____

_____

_____

_____

_____

_____

_____

_____

_____

_____

_____

_____

_____

_____

_____

_____

_____

WHO AM I?

_____

_____

_____

_____

_____

_____

_____

_____

_____

_____

_____

_____

_____

_____

_____

_____

_____

_____

_____

WHO AM I?

_____

_____

_____

_____

_____

_____

_____

_____

_____

_____

_____

_____

_____

_____

_____

_____

_____

WHY AM I HERE?

Answering the question of 'Why am I here?' involves discovering what is most important to us, especially in terms of the contribution we make to others. Use the questions below to guide you.

- Who are you making a contribution to?
- What impact will that contribution have on them?
- How will you make that contribution—Be specific.
- What does making that contribution give you?

Where there is more than one party that you're making a contribution to, capture each party separately.

WHY AM I HERE?

_____

_____

_____

_____

_____

_____

_____

_____

_____

_____

_____

_____

_____

_____

_____

_____

WHY AM I HERE?

_____

_____

_____

_____

_____

_____

_____

_____

_____

_____

_____

_____

_____

_____

_____

_____

WHY AM I HERE?

WHY AM I HERE?

HOW WILL I LEAD AND LIVE?

Answering the question of 'How will I lead and live?' involves exploring how we will act with greater mindful intention. Use the questions below to guide you.

Against what you've captured for 'Who am I?' and Why am I here?', identify:

- What current habits help or get in the way of you bringing to life your authentic identity and sense of purpose? In identifying these, consider what habits do you need to let go of and what further habits do you need to establish?
- What is your usual energy cycle through the day and week? When are you at your most and least energised and effective? What can you do to better manage your energy rather than your time?
- What distractions most heavily affect you? What can you do to eliminate these distractions?

HOW WILL I LEAD AND LIVE?

_____

_____

_____

_____

_____

_____

_____

_____

_____

_____

_____

_____

_____

_____

_____

_____

_____

_____

_____

_____

_____

_____

HOW WILL I LEAD AND LIVE?

HOW WILL I LEAD AND LIVE?

HOW WILL I LEAD AND LIVE?

_____

_____

_____

_____

_____

_____

_____

_____

_____

_____

_____

_____

_____

_____

_____

_____

MY STORY

Creating your story involves bringing together your answers to 'The 3 Questions'™ into a simple definition of how you will lead and live with greater authenticity, purpose and mindful intention. Use the statements below to guide you.

- I am …
- Why I'm here is …
- How I will lead and live is …

MY STORY

MY STORY

MY STORY

MY STORY

_____

_____

_____

_____

_____

_____

_____

_____

_____

_____

_____

_____

_____

_____

_____

_____

_____

NOTES

1   Whyte, D. (2001). *Crossing the Unknown Sea: Work as a Pilgrimage of Identity*. New York: Riverhead Books. p. 73.

2   https://trainingindustry.com/wiki/outsourcing/size-of-training-industry/

3   Friedman, T.L. (2006). *Thank You for Being Late: An Optimist's Guide to Thriving in the Age of Accelerations*. New York: Penguin Books.

4   Heidegger, M. (1962). *Being and Time*. Oxford: Blackwell Publishing.

5   Spinelli, E. (2015). *Practicing Existential Therapy: The Relational World*. London: Sage Publications.

6   Goffee, R. and Jones, G. (2006). *Why Should Anyone be Led by You? What it Takes to be an Authentic Leader*. Cambridge: Harvard Business School Press.

7   Friedman, T.L. (2006). *Thank You for Being Late: An Optimist's Guide to Thriving in the Age of Accelerations*. New York: Penguin Books. p. 169.

8   Becker, E. (1973). *The Denial of Death*, London: Souvenir Press.

9   Lawler, J. (2005). *The Essence of Leadership? Existentialism and leadership*. London: Sage Publications.

10 Frankl, V.E. (2006). *Man's Search for Meaning*. Boston: Beacon Press.

11 Jung, C.G. (1960). 'Synchronicity: An Acausal Connecting Principle', *The Structure and Dynamics of the Psyche*, Vol. 8 of *The Collected Works of C.G. Jung*, trans. R.F.C Hull. Princeton: Princeton University Press. p. 520

12 Clifford Nass, speaking to NPR's Ira Flatflow – https://www.npr.org/2013/05/10/182861382/the-myth-of-multitasking